本书获厦门理工学院外国语学院资助

OF TRANSFORMATION

化 书

（汉英对照）

［唐］谭 峭　著

朱玉敏　注译

世界图书出版公司

广州·上海·西安·北京

图书在版编目（CIP）数据

化书：汉英对照 /（唐）谭峭著；朱玉敏注译. —广州：世界图书出版广东有限公司，2022.12
ISBN 978-7-5192-5962-4

Ⅰ. ①化… Ⅱ. ①谭… ②朱… Ⅲ. ①古典哲学—中国—五代十国时期—汉、英 ②道家—汉、英 ③《道德经》—注释 ④《道德经》—译文 Ⅳ. ①B241.8 ②B223.12

中国版本图书馆CIP数据核字（2022）第244107号

书　　名	化书（汉英对照）	
	HUASHU（HANYING DUIZHAO）	
著　　者	[唐] 谭　峭	
注 译 者	朱玉敏	
策划编辑	刘正武	
责任编辑	魏志华	
装帧设计	书窗设计	
责任技编	刘上锦	
出版发行	世界图书出版有限公司　世界图书出版广东有限公司	
地　　址	广州市海珠区新港西路大江冲25号	
邮　　编	510300	
电　　话	020-84184026　84453623	
网　　址	http://www.gdst.com.cn	
邮　　箱	wpc_gdst@163.com	
经　　销	各地新华书店	
印　　刷	广州市迪桦彩印有限公司	
开　　本	787 mm×1 092 mm　1/16	
印　　张	16.25	
字　　数	453千字	
版　　次	2022年12月第1版　　2022年12月第1次印刷	
国际书号	ISBN 978-7-5192-5962-4	
定　　价	65.00元	

谭峭幼读经史，属文清丽。父唐国子司业①洙，训以进士业，而峭爱好黄老②、诸子及《穆天子传》③《汉武帝内传》④《茅君列仙内传》⑤等书，立志修道学仙。后辞父出游终南山、太白山、太行山、王屋山、嵩山、华山、泰山⑥等名山而不复返。其父驰书责之，乃复信曰："茅君昔为人子亦辞父学仙，今峭慕之，冀其有益。"父知其求道心坚，亦无可奈何；而心常念之，每遣家童⑦寻访，并寄以衣物钱帛。峭将父所寄衣赠贫寒人家，钱帛存放于酒肆。于嵩山师事道士十余年，得辟谷⑧、养气之术。

惟以酒为乐，常处醉乡中；夏日穿乌裘，冬著绿布衫，或整天卧于霜雪中，人以为已死，视之，呼吸如故。状类疯癫。每行吟诗曰："线作长江扇作天，靸鞋抛向海东边，蓬莱信道无多路，只在谭生拄杖前。"⑨据南唐沈汾《续仙传》载：谭峭后居南岳，炼丹⑩成，入水不濡，入火不灼，入青城⑪而去。

唐末五代社会动乱，谭峭不求仕进荣显，而以学道自隐。但他十分关心世道治乱，民生疾苦。乃著《化书》。他认为统治者的剥削、压迫，是

---

① 国子司业：属国子监的一个职位。国子监为中国古代的最高教育机构及教育管理部门。

② 黄老：中国战国时期兴起的哲学政治思想流派。黄指黄帝，老指老子。

③《穆天子传》：《穆天子传》分为六卷，记述了周穆王姬满游历天下之事。

④《汉武帝内传》：此书汉武帝出生时写起，直至死后殡葬。其中略于军政大事，而详于求仙问道。特别对西王母下降会武帝之事，描叙详尽。

⑤《茅君列仙内传》：一本描述道教求丹问仙的书。

⑥ 终南山、太白山、太行山、王屋山、嵩山、华山、泰山：皆为中国名山，山上众多庙宇，为道士仙人求丹问仙的圣地。

⑦ 家童：又作"家僮"旧时对私家奴仆的统称。

⑧ 辟谷：即不吃五谷杂粮，而以药食等其他之物充腹，或在一定时间内断食，是古人常用的一种养生方式。

⑨ 线作长江扇作天，靸鞋抛向海东边，蓬莱信道无多路，只在谭生拄杖前。线可以当作长江，扇子可以当作天。靸鞋不想要了可以扔到海东边。去蓬莱的路并没有多长，都在我的拄杖前吧。

此诗主要表达谭峭一种无为、豁达的性格。蓬莱指代道，而道并不远，就在心里。

⑩ 丹：道教上中一种可以治病、使人长生不老的药。

⑪ 青城：青城派是道教内丹修炼的派别。

造成人民痛苦，社会动乱的基本原因，统治者的骄奢淫逸、享乐腐化，是加重剥削压迫，激化社会矛盾的内在因素；提出统治者应用道化、术化、德化、仁化、食化、俭化，以医治社会弊病，实现天下太平。这在一定程度上反映了人民企求安定生活的愿望。

谭峭本老庄思想，认为世界万事万物皆源于虚，"虚化神，神化气，气化形"，复归于虚。他写成《化书》后，交南唐宋齐丘，请其作序传世。宋齐丘遂占为有，一时《化书》被名为《齐丘子》，以致南唐沈汾《续仙传》为谭峭立传时未述及撰《化书》事。后陈抟揭露宋齐丘欺世盗名的丑行，称："吾师友谭景升始于终南山著《化书》，因游三茅，经历建康（今江苏南京），见齐丘，……乃出《化书》授齐丘曰：'是书之化，其化无穷，愿子序之，流于后世'，于是杖锡而去。齐丘夺为己有而序之耳。"自此，始正名为《谭子化书》，或称《化书》。元人赵道一编纂《历世真仙体道通鉴》的谭峭传，即在《续仙传》的基础上补叙了陈景元所述陈抟揭露宋齐丘夺《化书》一事。

《化书》通篇讲"化"的内容，认为道在天地不可见，能见到的是道的转化；这个转化也不可见，见到的是转化出的具体形态。清气化为天，浊气化为地，中和之气化为人，斑杂之气化为万物。气化生成万物，反过来万物消亡化为气，无始无终，循环不已。全书有相互关联的六部分：道、术、德、仁、食、俭。道为虚无，无以自守，于是用术来补其不足；术为虚无之窍，飘渺间无可显，唯神气可用之，于是用德来补其不足；德为清净，无法体现出来，用仁来补其不足；仁为博爱，空洞无实，因此用食来补其不足；食为民之天，是出现社会动荡的根本原因，用俭来补其不足。这样，六卷转化依次展开，成为化书。

《化书》阐述了谭峭的哲学思想。他将道家的"虚无"理论进一步推进，认为一切来源于虚无，又最终归于虚无。他的这种思想，可以说是对道教中变化理论的最全面的发展。另外，他主张无形、无影、无寒、无暑、无生、无死、齐昏明、齐奢检……。他盼望的是一个"无亲、无疏、无爱、无恶"的"太和"社会，虽然这在当时的封建社会无法实现，但体现了他的崇高理想。对我们现代社会也有很好的警示作用。

Translator's Preface

Tan Qiao was was fond of reading scriptures and historical books since he was still a child, and his articles are clear, elegant and beautiful. His father, Tan Zhu by name, worked as a *Guo Zi Si Ye*[1] in Tang Dyansty, who wanted to train his son to be a scholar and then in the end to be an official, however, Tan Qiao was only interested in the thoughts of *Huang Lao*[2] and other philosophers, and he was obsessed with the philosophical books such as *Tale of King Mu, Son of Heaven*[3], *The Biography of Emperor Wu of Han*[4] and *The Biography of Mao and other Immortals*[5], etc, and aspired to get the essence of Taoism and to be immortal. Later, he bade farewell to his father and went on a trip to *Zhongnan Mountain*, *Taibai Mountain*, Taihang Mountain, Wangwu Mountain, Songshan Mountain, Huashan Mountain, Taishan Mountain[6] and other famous mountains and never returned. His father wrote a letter to rebuke him, and he replied: "Mao Jun is also a son who bade farewell to his father to study the way to be immortal. I now admire him, and want to be like him, hoping that it would be beneficial." Tang Qiao's father realized that he was determined to seek the Way of Taoism, but he could do nothing about it. He missed and thought about

---

[1] Guo Zi Si Ye: A position in Guo Zi Jian, which is the highest educational institution and educational administrative agency in ancient China.

[2] Huang Lao: A school of philosophical and political thought that emerged during the Warring States period in China. Huang refers to the Yellow Emperor and Lao refers to Laozi.

[3] Tale of King Mu, Son of Heaven: One of the historical books of the Western Zhou Period. The book is divided into six volumes, describing the travels of King Mu of the Zhou Dynasty—Ji Man, around the world.

[4] "The Biography of Emperor Wu of Han": This book depicts Emperor Wu of the Han Dynasty from his birth to his funeral. It skims over the military and political events, but goes into detail on the quest for immortality. In particular, the story of the descent of the Queen Mother of the West to meet Emperor Wu of the Han Dynasty is described in detail. It is rather of a book on Taoism than on history.

[5] "The Biography of Mao and other Immortals": A book on Taoism.

[6] Zhongnan Mountain, Taibai Mountain, Taihang Mountain, Wangwu Mountain, Songshan Mountain, Huashan Mountain, Taishan Mountain: These are all famous mountains in China with many temples where the Taoist Priests study the mystery of the universe and the methods to be immortal.

his son, Tan Qiao, all the time, and often sent the private servants to take clothes and money to him. However, Tan Qiao immediately gave the clothes away to the poor, and stored the money in a wine shop. He studied with a Taoist priest in Songshan Mountain for more than ten years, learning Pi Gu[1] and Qi[2] Nourishment.

He had great love for wine, and was often deadly drunk. In summer, he wore black furs; while in winter, he wore coarse shirts. Sometimes, he laid in frost and snow all day long, and people nearby thought he must have been dead, but when they checked him closely, they found that he was still breathing. He looked like a madman, and often chanted poems while walking: *"The line for Yangtze River and the fan for the sky, Ji Shoes thrown to the east of the sea. The way to Penglai is not long, it's only in front of Tang Qiao's crutches."*[3] According to Shen Fen's *The Sequel to the Legend of the Immortals* in the Southern Tang Dynasty, "Tan Qiao lived in Nanyue after he succeeded in refining the Dan[4], after which water couldn't moisten him and fire couldn't burn him and he became a member of the school of Qingcheng[5]."

During the social turmoil of the late Tang and Five Dynasties, Tan Qiao did not seek to pursue glory and scholarly prominence, but to live in seclusion and learn Taosim. However, he was much concerned about the governance of the ruling class and the hardships of the people. Therefore, he wrote the book of "Transformation" in six volumes which include one hundred and ten articles. He believed that the exploitation and oppression by the rulers were the basic causes of people's sufferings and social unrest, and that the arrogance, extravagance and corruption of the rulers were the inherent factors that aggravated the exploitation and oppression and intensified social conflicts; he proposed that the rulers should apply morality, art, virtue, benevolence, food and frugality to cure social ills and

---

①Pi Gu: Food fasting: It is also called stop diet. It is a common way for the ancients to maintain their health by not eating grains or cereals, and they would relieve their hunger by having traditional Chinese herbs, or they would fast for a certain period of time.

②Qi: It refers to Yuanqi — literally means the original energy, and it refers to the original substance that produces and constitutes all things in heaven and earth.

③Meaning of the poem: A line can be deemed as Yangtze River and a fan as the sky. Ji Shoes (a type of slippers in Ancient China which is made of cloth), if not wanted, can be thrown to the east of the sea. Penglai represents the realm of Taoism's gods and immortals. In short, it means that the highest realm pursued by Taoism is not in Penglai, but is actually in your heart.

④Dan: It refers to the elixir that the Taoists pursue, which is believed to cure illnesses and to make people live forever.

⑤Qingcheng: It refers to a school of Taoism, and it mainly focuses on refining elixir.

achieve peace in the world. To a certain extent, it reflected the people's desire for a stable life.

The thoughts of Tan Qiao are based on those of Laozi[①], and he believed that everything in the world originates from Nothingness and that "Nothingness turns into god, god into Qi, Qi into form", and finally returns to Nothingness. After he wrote the book *Of Transformation*, he gave it to Song Qiqiu, one of his best friends of the Southern Tang Dynasty and asked him to write a preface to it. However, Song Qiqiu took the book as his own and renamed it "Qiqiu Zi". For this reason, when the biography of Tan Qiao was written by Shen Fen of the Southern Tang Dynasty in his *The Sequel to the Legend of the Immortals*, Tan Qiao's *Of Transformation* was not mentioned. Later, Chen Tuan exposed the scandalous act of Song Qiqiu in deceiving the world and stealing Tang Qiao's name, saying: "My teacher and friend Tan Qiao wrote the book *Of Transformation* in Zhongnan Mountain, and on his way to Mao Mountain, he passed by Jiankang, where he met Qiqiu, ... and gave him the book and said, "This book is about transformation, which is infinite. You may preface it, and let the name of the book be immortalized." Then he left with his crutch. Qiqiu appropriated book as that of his own and prefaced it." After this exposure, this book was renamed "Transformation by Tanzi" or "Transformation". Zhao Daoyi of the Yuan dynasty added the event that Song Qiqiu took *Of Transformation* as that of his own when he compiled the biography of Tan Qiao in his book *General Guide to the True Immortals of All Ages*, which was based on the *The Sequel to the Legend of the Immortals*.

Transformation is a Taoist book written by Tan Qiao of the Five Dynasties, which contains a unique understanding of Taoism. Throughout the book, he talks about "transformation", arguing that the Tao is invisible in this world, and that what can be seen is the transformation of Tao. This transformation is also invisible, and what can be seen is the specific form of the transformation. Clear Qi is transformed into heaven, turbid Qi is transformed into earth, neutral Qi is transformed into human beings, and mottled Qi is transformed into all things. Qi is transformed into all things, and in turn, all things perish and become Qi, without beginning and without end. There are altogether six related volumes — *Tao*, *Art*, *Benevolence*, *Virtue*, *Food*, *Frugality*. Tao is from Nothingness, and there is no way to guard itself, so it is supplemented by Art; Art is the trick of Nothingness,

---

①Laozi: Laozi is the most famous representative of Taoism.

and there is no way to show it in the ethereal, and only the divine Qi is available, so it is supplemented by Virtue; Virtue is purity, and it cannot be manifested, so it is supplemented by Benevolence; Benevolence is universal love, but it is empty and insubstantial, so it is supplemented by food; food is the heaven of the people, and it is the root cause of social unrest, so it is supplemented by frugality. In this way, the transformation in six volumes unfolds sequentially and becomes a book of transformation.

Of Transformation expounds Tan Qiao's philosophical thoughts. He takes the Taoist theory of "nothingness" one step further, arguing that everything comes from nothingness and ultimately returns to nothingness, which can be said to be the most comprehensive development of the theory of change in Taoism. In addition, he advocated the state of "formlessness", "shadowlessness", "coldlessness", "heatlessness", "birthlessness" and "deathlessness", a state where one can treat day and night, luxury and frugality as the same. He desired for a society of "Taihe" in which there would be "no relatives, no alienation, no love, and no hatred", which, though could not be realized in the feudal society at that time, reflected his lofty ideal, and it can also serve as a warning to our modern society.

目 录

卷二 术化 Volume 2 The Transformation of Arts

卷三　德化　Volume 3　The Transformation of the Virtues

卷四　仁化　Volume 4　The Transformation of Benevolence

卷五　食化　Volume 5　The Transformation of Food

卷六 俭化 Volume 6　The Transformation of Frugality

卷一
Volume 1

道　化

The Transformation of Tao

化书之 1

·原文·

道① 化

　　道之委也，虚化神，神化气②，气化形，形生而万物所以塞也。道之用也，形化气，气化神，神化虚，虚明而万物所以通也。是以古圣人穷通塞之端，得造化之源，忘形以养气，忘气以养神，忘神以养虚。虚实相通，是谓大同③。故藏之为元精④，用之为万灵⑤，含之为太一⑥，放之为太清⑦。是以坎离⑧消长于一身，风云⑨发泄于七窍，真气薰蒸而时无寒暑，纯阳流注而民无死生，是谓神化之道者也。

---

①道：是道教的主题词。字面意思讲就是道路。在道教中，道是万物存在的源头及推动力。

②气：指元气。指产生和构成天地万物的原始物质。

③大同：天地万物与人合而为一，此处指达到虚实统一的一种境界，指与大道融为一体。

④元精：意思是指天地的精气，人体的精气。元气为万物之本原，是指构成人体的基本物质，也是人体生长发育及各种功能活动的物质基础。元精与元气的关系非常密切。元精乃元气之"精英"，由"元气之积厚"而生，此即谓"气归精"。

⑤万灵：众生灵；人类。此处指元精之妙用，发挥于外。

⑥太一：又指宇宙万物的本原、本体，也可以指天地万物的元气。

⑦太清：古人指元气之清者。

⑧坎：以道家解释，坎为肾，为水，为气，为铅，为阴；离：为心，为火，为神，为汞，为阳。"坎离消长于一身"，即一身之阴阳前降而后升。

⑨风云：即人之身之中升而为阳，降而为阴。散之于百骸，发之于七窍。

道　化

　　道的顺序转化，是由虚无中产生精神和意识，精神和意识中产生孕育个体的元气，元气凝聚转化形成形体。个体的形状各不相同，因而世间万物各不相同。道的逆序转化，则是由个体形态转化为元气，元气转化为精神和意识，精神和意识回归虚无，在虚无中没有形态的差别，所以万物相通。古代先贤至圣探究万物相隔而又相通的根源，明白了万物如何创造出来和进行转化的原理。因此，他们忘掉自己的形体存在，专心培养自身元气，而后，忘掉元气专心滋养精神和意识，最后忘掉精神和意识，进入虚无境界。虚无和形体之间的转化如果能够畅通，就可以称之为达到了大道圆融的状态。因此，把大道收藏在内就化为元精，把大道运用在外就化为万灵，内外结合就化为太一，释放开来就化为太清。于是坎离在自己全身升降，风云从七窍之中发散，元气薰化蒸腾，四时就没有严寒或酷暑；纯粹的阳气流动施注，百姓就没有生死之忧了。这就叫作神化之道。

Chapter 1

The Transformation of Tao[①]

The sequential transformation of Tao is like this—out of nothingness comes spirit and

---

①Tao: It is a key word in Taoism. Literally speaking, Tao means way or path. In Taoism, it denotes something that is both the source of and the force behind everything in this world.

consciousness, and out of spirit and consciousness comes Qi① that nurtures the individual, which coalesces and transforms into the individual, which, in its many different shapes, forms the diverse and colorful material world. The transformation of Tao in reverse order is like this—out of individual forms comes Yuanqi, which in turn is transformed into spirit and consciousness, and they then return to nothingness, in which all things are the same and all things are essentially connected. The ancient sages and saints examined in great depth the cyclical process of all things from their creation to their return to nature and the reasons why things are the same in nature while different in forms, and they finally understood the principles behind it—how all things are created and transformed. Therefore, they forget their own physical existence and concentrate on cultivating their own Yuanqi, and then forget their Yuanqi and concentrate on nourishing their spirit and consciousness, and they finally enter the realm of nothingness, forgetting even their own spirit and consciousness.

By communicating between nothingness and one's own body, one attains the harmonious state with Tao, which is commonly referred to as Great Harmony②. Thus,when Tao is hidden, it exists in one's body in the form of Yuanjing③; when manifested and applied excellently, it is in the form of Wanling④; when Yuanjing and Wanling are combined, it is in the state of Tai Yi⑤, and when Tai Yi is released outwardly, it is in the state of Tai Qing⑥. Yin-Yang⑦ and Water-fire in one's body conflict, and the Qi produced by these conflicts is released to the outside through the seven apertures (seven apertures refer to two nostrils, ears, eyes and mouth on the human head), and the true Qi in the body is always fumigating

---

①Qi: It refers to Yuanqi—literally means the original energy, and it refers to the original substance that produces and constitutes all things in heaven and earth.

②Great Harmony: It generally refers to the condition that all things in heaven and earth are one with man, and here it describes a state of unity between things tangible and intangible, and in harmony with Tao.

③Yuanjing: In Taoism, Yuanjing means the essence of the heaven, the earth and the human body.It is the basic substance that constitutes the human body and is the material basis for growth and development and various functional activities of the human body. Yuanjing and Yuanqi are closely related. Yuanjing is the "elite" of the elemental energy and is the "accumulation of the Yuanqi", which is called the "return of Qi/Energy to Jing/essence".

④Wanling: All living things in the world including human beings. Here it refers to the great use of Yuanjing.

⑤Tai Yi: It refers to the origins and Yuanqi of all things in the world.

⑥Tai Qing: It refers to people whose Yuanqi is clean.

⑦Yin and Yang: In Taoism it means Kan and Li. Kan refers to the kidney, water, air, lead, and it is Yin; Li refers to the heart, fire, god, mercury, and it is Yang. "Kan and Li ebb and flow in one's body", that is, the Yin and Yang ebb and flow in one's body.When Qi flows in one's body, it is Yang, while when it ebbs, it is Yin.

the organs and bones, so that the hot and cold changes in the external climate have no effect on the body, and the true Qi keeps on flowing in and defending the whole body, so that the body functions with vitality and never ages, which is the way of the immortals.

化书之 2

·原文·

蛇 雀

蛇化为龟，雀[①]化为蛤[②]。彼忽然忘曲屈之状，而得蹒跚之质；此倏然失飞鸣之态，而得介甲之体。斫削不能加其功[③]，绳尺[④]不能定其象，何化之速也。且夫当空团块，见块而不见空；粉块求空，见空而不见块。形无妨而人自妨之，物无滞而人自滞之，悲哉！

·白话·

蛇和鸟雀

蛇变成乌龟，鸟雀变成蛤蚌。蛇忽然间忘却了自己原来身体蜿蜒曲折状态，变得行动缓慢、走路摇摆；鸟雀忽然间失去了飞翔和鸣叫的本能，换成了带甲壳的形体。即使刀削斧砍也不能形成这样的功效，用墨绳规尺也无法规定它的身体形状，这个转化速度是很快的。结成团的块状物遮蔽了天空，我们却只见到团块，而看不到天空，为了见到天空而把团块粉碎了以后，虽然见到了天空又但不见团块了。物体的外形并没有设置障碍，而人们却自己设置了障碍。万物之形体没有阻塞，人却自

---

①雀：泛指所有鸟。

②蛤：一种有壳的软体动物，生活江河湖海。

③加其功：形成那样的功效。

④绳尺：泛指一种计量单位。

己阻塞了自己。这是多么可悲的啊！

Chapter 2

Snakes and Birds

Snakes can become turtles, and birds can become clams. The snakes suddenly forget its originally sinuous shape of their bodies and get their currently slow, wobbly walks; the birds suddenly lose their instinctive nature of flying and chirping and are equipped with shells. Even knife-cutting cannot make the snakes or birds own these new functions, nor can any measuring instruments determine the shapes of their bodies, and these changes are quite rapid. When a big block made up of aggregated clods obscures the sky, what people can see is only the block, not the sky. In order to see the sky, people break the block. However, they now can only see the sky, yet not the block.The form of an object does not set up obstacles, but people set up obstacles themselves. The forms of all things are not obstructed, but man obstructs themselves. The forms of all things in the world are transformable without any blocks, but people block themselves. How sad this is!

化书之 **3**

·原文·

老 枫

老枫化为羽人①，朽麦化为蝴蝶，自无情而之有情也。贤女化为贞石②，山蚯③化为百合，自有情而之无情也。是故土木金石④，皆有情性精魄。虚无所不至，神无所不通，气无所不同，形无所不类。孰为彼，孰为我？孰为有识，孰为无识？万物，一物也；万神，一神也，斯道之至矣。

·白话·

老 枫

古老的枫树变成了身上长有羽毛的仙人，腐朽的麦粒变成了蝴蝶，这是从没性情到有性情的转变。贤良的女子变成了坚硬的石头，山中的蚯蚓变成了百合花，这是由有性情到没有性情的转变。因此，无论土壤、树木、金属、石头，都有禀赋和气质、精气和魂魄。任何地方都有虚无的存在，精神都是无所不通的、元气也都是相同的，形体也都可以归为一类。哪个是他，哪个是我？哪个是有见识的，哪个是

---

①羽人：神话中有羽翼的仙人。道家学仙而飞升，因称道士为羽人。

②贞石：坚硬的石头。

③山蚯：即山中蚯蚓。

④土木金石：泛指自然界中的物品。

无见识的？万物其实就是一物，万神其实就是一神，这就是道的极致了。

Chapter **3**

The Old Maple Tree

The old maple tree becomes a flying fairy with feathers[1], and the rotten wheat becomes a butterfly. This is the transformation from the lack of intelligence and emotion to the presence of intelligence and emotion. The virtuous woman turns into a hard stone, and the earthworm turns into a flower of lily. This is the transformation from the presence of intelligence and emotion to the lack of intelligence and emotion.Thus, whether it is soil, tree, metal or stone, they all have spirits, temperaments, energy and soul. There is nothingness everywhere, and out of nothingness comes spirit and consciousness,which are all alike, and out of spirit and consciousness comes Yuanqi that conceives each individual, which are the same, and the forms of different individual in the world is similar in the early stages of conception and can be classified into one same type. Therefore, how can we tell which one is me and which one is not, or who is the one with intelligence and who is the one without? All things are one thing, and all gods are one god, and this is the perfect expression of Taoism.

---

[1] It refers to immortals with feathers in mythology. In Taoism, Taoists get Tao and ascend to the heaven, and they are also called immortals.

· 原文 ·

耳 目

目所不见，设明镜而见之；耳所不闻，设虚器①而闻之。精神在我，视听在彼。骈趾②可以割，陷吻③可以补，则是耳目可以妄设，形容可以伪置。既假又假，既惑又惑。所以知魂魄魅我，血气醉我，七窍④囚我，五根⑤役我。惟神之有形，由形之有疣。苟无其疣，何所不可？

· 白话 ·

耳 目

眼睛无法看到的地方，借助明亮的镜子就可以看得到；耳朵听不到的声音，借助中空的器物就可以听得到。看与不看、听与不听决定于自己的意识，看见的和听到的东西决定于镜子和助听的器物。脚趾并趾相连，可以切割开来恢复正常；嘴唇缺陷，也可以修补。因此，所见所闻可以虚构。外表形貌可以进行伪装。这样一而

---

① 虚器：中空的器物，可使进入的声音放大。
② 骈趾：足大拇趾与第二指相连为一趾的畸形。
③ 陷吻：裂唇。
④ 七窍：眼、耳、口、鼻七孔。
⑤ 五根：即视觉、听觉、嗅觉、味觉、触觉之五官及其机能。

再、再而三的造假，自己也不断的被这些假的东西所迷惑。由此可知，人的本性被深受生活习气感染的魂魄所引诱，被身体血气运行状态所迷醉，被眼睛、耳朵、鼻子、嘴巴所囚禁，受到视觉、听觉、嗅觉、味觉、触觉的奴役。人的精神和意识受到形体的限制，就像身体上有疣子一样。假如精神和意识能够摆脱形体的束缚，就像身体没有了疣子一样，那还有什么办不到的事情呢？

Chapter 4

The Eyes and the Ears

What the eye cannot see can be seen with the help of a mirror; what the ear cannot hear can be heard with the help of a hollow object[①]. Whether one wants to see or not and whether one wants to hear or not are determined by one's own consciousness, and the things one sees and hears are determined by the mirrors and aids to hearing.

For deformities where the big toe of the foot is joined to the second toe as one toe, the toe can be restored to the normal state by cutting it open with a knife, and for deformities where the lip is split, the opening can be surgically filled in. This shows that the hearing and seeing of the ears and eyes can be achieved at will, and the outward form can be disguised. In this way everything can be repeatedly falsified, and one is constantly confused by these falsehoods. This led me to understand that human nature is seduced by a soul deeply infected by the habits of life, intoxicated by the state of operation of the body's blood, imprisoned by the eyes, ears, nose and mouth, and enslaved by the senses of sight, hearing, smell, taste and touch. But every human spirit and consciousness has a form, just as the body has warts on it. If spirit and consciousness are free from the bondage of form, just as the body is free from warts, what could not be done?

---

① Hollow objects can also be called hollow artifacts that can amplify the incoming sound.

化书之 **5**

·原文·

环　舞①

作环舞者宫室皆转，瞰迴流者头目自旋。非宫室之幻惑也，而人自惑之；非迴流之改变也，而人自变之。是故粉巾②为兔，药石③为马，而人不疑；甘言巧笑，图脸画眉，而人不知。唯清静者，物不能欺。

·白话·

环　舞

舞蹈的人在做旋转动作时，会觉得周围的房屋都在旋转，俯身向下看山涧中水流时，会觉得头晕目眩。并非是房屋使人产生旋转的幻觉，而是人自己心里生出的幻觉；并非是水流使人头晕目眩，而是人自己心里生出头晕目眩的幻觉。因此，把白巾结成兔子状，把药石做成马形，人们却不加怀疑。让它们说好话，让它们发出诱人的笑声，粉饰它们的容貌，描绘它们的眉目，可是人们却不知道。只有心地清净的人，才能不被事物的表面现象所迷惑。

---

① 环舞：旋转动作的舞蹈。
② 粉巾：白巾。
③ 药石：古时指冶病的药物和砭石。

The Dancing Move of Spinning

When a dancer does a dancing move of spinning, he feels that the house is spinning with him, and when a person leans down to look at the water flowing down the mountain, he feels dizzy. It is not the house or water that gives one the illusion of spinning, but the illusion in one's own mind that makes one dizzy. When the white scarves are knotted in the shape of rabbits and the medicinal stones[①] are carved in the shape of horses, people do not suspect. Furthermore, when they are put on make-ups, and made to speak good words, nobody is aware of it. Only those who are pure and peaceful in heart cannot be confused by the superficial appearance of things.

①medicinal stones: In ancient times, it refers to the medicine and stone used to cure diseases.

化书之 **6**

原文

铅 丹①

术有火练铅丹以代谷食者，其必然也。然岁丰则能饱，岁俭则能饥，是非丹之恩，盖由人之诚②也。则是我本不饥而自饥之，丹本不饱而自饱之。饥者大妄③，饱者大幻④，盖不齐其道也。故人能一有无，一死生，一情性，一内外，则可以蜕五行⑤、脱三光⑥，何患乎一日百食，何虑乎百日一食。

白话

铅丹

在道术中有一种炼丹之术，所炼的丹可以替代五谷为食物，这是理所当然的事情。然而在丰收年景丹能够让人吃饱，歉收年景丹不能够让人吃饱，并非是由于丹的功效真的如此，而是由于人的心理信念决定的。于是本来并不饥饿，由于心里不相信能吃饱，因而感到饥饿，丹本来并不能使我吃饱，由于心里相信它能让我饱，就感到已经饱了。感到饥饿的人总是处于自己不能吃饱的妄想之中，感到饱食的人

---

① 铅丹：即道家所炼成的丹药，可入药。依道家之说，铅丹可代五谷，服后不饥。
② 诚：诚心。
③ 大妄：非分之想。
④ 大幻：虚幻的感觉。
⑤ 五行：水、火、木、金、土，道教指构成各种物质的五种元素。
⑥ 三光：日、月、星。

总是处在自己已经吃饱的幻想中，这都是因为他们不能和道合二为一。因此，人若是能够将有与无，生与死，情与性，内与外统一，就可以跳出金木水火土五行的约束，摆脱对日月星三光的依赖，既不会为一日吃百餐而发愁，也不会为百天只能吃一餐而忧愁了。

Chapter 6

Qian Dan[①]

In Taoism there is the art of alchemy(the process of making Qian Dan), and it is only logical that the Qian Dan can replace the grains as food. However, in good years Qian Dan can fill people up and in bad years Qian Dan cannot, not because Dan is really effective, but because of one's piety and sincerity. So people are in fact not hungry, but they feel hungry because they do not believe in their heart that they can be full. Although Qian Dan does not fill them up, they feel full because they believe in their heart that it would fill them up. He who feels hungry is always in the delusion that he cannot be full, and he who feels full is always under the illusion that he is already full, and these are due to their deviations from Tao. Therefore, if one can merge one's tangible self with the formless and phantom nothingness, one's death with one's new birth, one's emotion with one's nature, and the interior of one's body with one's exterior, one can break out of the constraints of Wuxing[②] of Metal, Wood, Water, Fire and Earth. At this moment, one can be free from the dependence on the Three Lights[③] of the sun, the moon and the stars, and will not worry about a hundred meals a day, or a meal in a hundred days.

---

①Qian Dan: It refers to the elixir in Taoism that is believed to cure illnesses or to make people live forever.According to Taoism, Qian Dan can replace grains as food and men will not feel hungry after having it.

②Wuxing: It refers to water, fire, wood, metal and earth, which in Taosim is believed to make up various substances.

③Three Lights: The earth, the moon and the stars.

化书之 7

形 影

以一镜照形，以余镜照影。镜镜相照，影影相传，不变冠剑①之状，不夺黼黻②之色。是形也与影无殊，是影也与形无异。乃知形以非实，影以非虚，无实无虚，可与道俱。

形 影

使用一面镜子来照自己的形体，用其他的镜子来照这一只镜子中的影像，镜子之间互相照映，影像在这些镜子中依次传递，影像的衣冠配饰丝毫不变，服饰上精美的花纹色泽丝毫不减。真实的形体与影像看起来没有差别，镜子中的影像与真实的形体看起来也毫无区别。通过这些，我们明白，形体可以并非实体，影像也可以并非虚像。若能达到实体和虚体的和谐统一，就与道的本质相符合了。

①冠剑：冠巾和佩剑，这里代指人之装束。
②黼黻（fǔ fú）：古代礼服上绘绣的花纹，这里亦代指人之装束。

Forms and Images

One mirror is used to look at one's own form, and other mirrors are used to look at the image in this one mirror, and the image is passed through these mirrors in turn, with the image's clothing and accessories remaining unchanged and the fine embroidered patterns[1] on the clothing unchanged. There is no difference between the real form and the image, and the image in the mirror appears to be the same as the real form. It is thus clear that a tangible form can have an intangible appearance and an image can have a physical form. If one can achieve harmony between the the tangible and the intangible, one can grasp the essence of Tao.

---

[1]embroidered patterns: It refers to the embroidered patterns on decent clothes in ancient times, and it is also used here to refer to the attire of people.

化书之 **8**

·原文·

蛰 藏①

物有善于蛰藏者，或可以御大寒，或可以去大饥，或可以万岁不死。以其心冥冥②兮无所知，神怡怡兮无所之，气熙熙无所为。万虑不能惑，求死不可得。是以大人③体物知身，体身知神，体神知真，是谓吉人之津。

·白话·

蛰 藏

善于蛰藏的动物，有的在蛰藏状态下，可以抵御严寒，有的可以消除饥饿，有的可以生活一万年都不会死。在蛰藏状态下，这些动物心思此时昏暗不明，对任何事情都没有知觉和反应，精神和意识怡然自得，不会偏移；生命的元气平静、温和、欢乐，不愿有任何作为。这种状态下，任何的思虑都不能使之迷惑，即使想结束自己的生命也无法办到。于是德行高尚、志趣高远的人通过动物蛰藏作用的启发，领悟了自己身体的能力，通过自己身体的能力的启迪，领悟了自己精神和意识的意义，通过自己精神和意识的意义的启发，领悟了道的涵义。蛰藏可以说是人通往幸福的途径。

---

①蛰藏：即昆虫等动物的蛰居、潜藏。
②冥冥：指昏昧的状态。
③大人：德行高尚、志趣高远的人

Chapter **8**

Hibernation

Among the animals that are good at hibernation, some can withstand the cold, some can endure hunger, and some can live extremely long lives. In the state of hibernation, the mind of these animals is in a state of meditation, unaware of and unresponsive to anything. Their spirit and consciousness are at ease, unconcerned with their place and state, and their Yuanqi are at peace and quiet, not doing anything. In this state, no concerns can bother them, and even if they wanted to end their lives, they could not do so. Thus through the enlightenment of the animal's hibernating process, the wise man comprehends the power of one's body, which in turn reveals to him the meaning of his spirit and consciousness, and it in the end leads to the meaning of the Tao. Therefore, the hibernating process can be described as the the way to blessings for the blessed.

·原文·

枭[1] 鸡

枭夜明而昼昏，鸡昼明而夜昏，其异同也如是。或谓枭为异，则谓鸡为同；或谓鸡为异，则谓枭为同。孰枭鸡之异昼夜乎？昼夜之异枭鸡乎？枭鸡之同昼夜乎？夫耳中磬[2]，我自闻；目中花，我自见。我之昼夜，彼之昼夜，则是昼不得谓之明，夜不得谓之昏。能齐昏明者，其唯大人乎！

·白话·

枭 鸡

猫头鹰夜晚有精神，出来活动，而白天却不清醒、睡大觉，雄鸡相反，白天精神出来活动而夜晚睡大觉，他们的异同就是如此。如果说猫头鹰为不正常的，那么，雄鸡就是正常的；如果说雄鸡是不正常的，那么，猫头鹰就是正常的了。判断猫头鹰和雄鸡之间谁是不正常的标准是昼夜吗？判断昼夜之间谁是不正常的标准是猫头鹰和雄鸡吗？判断猫头鹰和雄鸡之间谁是正常的标准是昼夜吗？耳朵内的钟磬声音，只有自己才能听得见，自己心目中的花朵，只有自己才能看得见。因此，对于我的

[1] 枭：猫头鹰。
[2] 磬：一种古代的乐器，石头制成，通过敲击获取音乐声。

昼夜和其他人昼夜的判别，不能说白天就是明亮的，夜晚就是昏暗的。能够把昏明昼夜视为一个整体的，只有德行高尚、志趣高远的人。

Chapter 9

The Owl and the Rooster

The owl comes out at night and sleeps during the day, while the rooster comes out during the day and sleeps at night, and they are always so whether they are deemed normal or abnormal. If the owl is abnormal, then the rooster is normal; if the rooster is abnormal, then the owl is normal. Is day or night the criterion for determining which is normal or abnormal between an owl and a rooster? Is an owl or a rooster the criterion for determining which is abnormal between day and night? The sound of the Qing[1] chimes within one's ears can only be heard by oneself, and the flowers in one's mind can only be seen by oneself. Therefore, one cannot simply discern day from night by saying that day is bright and night is dark. The only people who can merge darkness with brightness are those who are virtuous and have great aspirations.

[1] Qing: It is a type of traditional Chinese musical instrument made of stones, and the music is made by tapping the stones.

·原文·

四　镜

小人常有四镜①：一名璧②，一名珠，一名砥③，一名盂④。璧视者大，珠视者小，砥视者正，盂视者倒。观彼之器，察我之形，由是无大小、无长短、无妍⑤丑、无美恶。所以知形气諂我，精魄贼我，奸臣贵我，礼乐尊我。是故心不得为之君心，王不得为之主。戒之如火，防之如虎。纯俭不可袭，清静不可侮，然后可以迹容广⑥而跻三五。

·白话·

四　镜

我自己经常以四个物件为镜子：一个是玉璧，一个是珠子，一个是磨石，一个是钵盂。玉璧看起来比较大，珠子则看起来比较小；磨石看起来是突起的，是正的，

---

① 四镜：四种可以察照之的东西。

② 璧：平圆形、中心有孔的玉器。

③ 砥：磨石，细为砥，粗为砺。

④ 盂：盛汤浆或食物之器皿。

⑤ 妍：美好。

⑥ 容广：容指容成。广：即广成子，都是广传上古时代的仙人。这里泛指德行高尚的圣人。

钵盂看起来则是凹空的，是倒置的。通过对这些器物的观察，再对比看看自己的形体，于是在心中同等对待万物，没有大与小的区别，没有长与短的区别，没有美与丑的区别，没有善与恶的区别。所以我明白，身体的体形和体内气血制约我，受生活习性熏染的魂魄在惑乱我，心怀叵测的人讨好我，国家的各种规章制度维护我。因此，心不能成为自己的心，就像国王不能成为一国之主。应该时刻保持警戒性，就像时刻保持对火灾的警戒一样；应该做好预防，就像防止老虎对人的伤害一样。这样，对身体内外的欲望和要求减少到最低，任何伤害都无法侵袭到自己；保持清净无为的状态，任何侮辱都无法降临到自己身上。随后，这样道德高深的事迹就广为流传并为众人所尊崇，从而跻身于荣成或者广成子这种德高望重的圣人之列。

Chapter 10

Four Mirrors[1]

I myself often use four objects as mirrors: the jade[2], the bead, the Di[3] and the Yu[4]. The jade looks bigger, the bead looks smaller; the Di is protruding and upright, while the Yu is hollow and upside down. By observing the images reflected from these objects and comparing my own form with these images, I then treat all things all alike in my mind, be they large or small, long or short, beautiful or ugly, good or evil. So I came to realize that the physical form and Qi within my body constrain me, the soul imbued with the habits of

---

①Four Mirrors: It refers to four objects that can be used to reflect the image of things, and they refer to the jade, bead, Di and Yu respectively.

②Jade: It refers to the round jade with a hole in the middle.

③Di: A type of grinding stone in Ancient China.

④Yu: Utensils for soup or food.

life confuses me, that people with evil intentions please me, and that the various rules and regulations of the state protect me. Therefore, the mind cannot be its own mind, just as an emperor cannot be the lord of a country. People should always be on guard, just as they are always on guard against fire; they should take precautions, just as a tiger is prevented from doing harm to a person. In this way, desires and demands, both inside and outside the body, are reduced to a minimum, and no harm can invade one; and by remaining pure and indifferent, no insult can befall one. Subsequently, people who have such deeds of great morality will be widely known and revered by all, and thus will rank among the saints of high virtue.

·原文·

射　虎

射似虎者，见虎而不见石；斩暴蛟者，见蛟而不见水。是知万物可以虚，我身可以无。以我之无，合彼之虚。自然可以隐可以显，可以死，可以生而无所拘。夫空中之尘若飞雪，而目未尝见；穴中之蚁若牛斗，而耳未尝闻，况非见闻者乎！

·白话·

射　虎

用弓箭射老虎的猎人，在射箭的时候眼睛里只看见老虎，而看不见老虎所站立的石头；斩杀残暴蛟龙的勇士，眼睛里只看见蛟龙，而看不见蛟龙所在的水域。由此便可知，你可将万物视作虚无，视而不见，自己的本身也可当作不存在。将自己身体的虚无与外物的虚无融为一体，就可以隐藏形体，也可以将形体显现出来；可以生、也可以死（一种状态，既可以朝气蓬勃、也可以毫无生气）。随心所欲，不拘一格。空气中的尘埃像雪花一般在空中飘散，而我们的眼睛却看不见；蚁穴中的蚂蚁像牛那样轰轰烈烈地争斗，而我们的耳朵却听不到，更何况那些我们未曾亲眼看到的事物，未曾亲耳听到的声音呢。

Chapter 11

Shoot the Tiger

The hunter who shoots a tiger with his bow and arrow sees only the tiger in his eyes, but not the rock on which the tiger stands; the warrior who slays a brutal dragon sees only the dragon in his eyes, but not the water in which it stays. Through this fact, we find that all things can be regarded as being invisible (or nothingness, non-existent), and our own bodies can also be treated as being non-existent. By merging one's non-existent body with nothingness of the outside, one can naturally hide one's form or reveal it; one can make one's body appear lifeless or vigorous. Thus one can follow one's heart and be unconventional. The dust in the air drifts like flying snow, but our eyes cannot see it; ants fight inside an anthill like bulls, but our ears cannot hear it, not to mention the things we have not seen with our own eyes and sounds we have not heard with our own ears.

化书之 12

龙 虎

龙化虎变，可以蹈虚空，虚空非无也；可以贯金石，金石非有也。有无相通，物我相同。其生非始，其死非终。知此道者，形不可得毙，神不可得逝。

龙 虎

龙和虎的形体变化后，可以在虚不着力的空中踏行，那么就是说，虚空并非什么都没有；龙和虎的形体变化后，可以穿过金属和岩石，也就可以说金属和岩石并非是真实的实体。真实的形体和虚无相通，外物和自我融合一体。形体的诞生并非是意识的开始，而形体的死亡也并非是意识的终结。明白这样道理的人，形体不会死亡，意识不会消失。

Chapter 12

The Dragon and the Tiger

When the dragon and tiger change their forms, they can step through the void without force, which means that the void is not nothing; meanwhile, they can pass through metal and rock, which means that metal and rock are not real entities. There is a connection between the real form and nothingness, and the external object and the self of one merge into one. The birth of form is not the beginning of consciousness, and the death of form is not the end of consciousness. Whoever understands this, their forms will not die and consciousness not disappear.

化书之 13

·原文·

游 云

游云无质①，故五色②舍③焉；明镜无瑕，故万物象焉。谓水之含天也，必天之含水也。夫百步之外，镜则见人，人不见影，斯为验也。是知太虚之中无所不有，万耀④之内无所不见。则世人且知心仰寥廓⑤，而不知迹处虚空。寥廓无所间，神明且不远。是以君子常正其心，常俨⑥其容。则可以游泳于寥廓，交友于神明而无咎也。

·白话·

游 云

天上漂浮的云朵没有自己的底色，因此，五色都可以停留在上面，留下颜色；明亮的镜子上面没有一丁点的污渍，因此可以原封不动的照出世界万物的影像。说

---

① 质：底色、质地。这里指游动的浮云，没有底色。
② 五色：青、黄、赤、白、黑，旧时把这五种颜色作为主要颜色。
③ 舍：保留。
④ 万耀：指日、月、星所照耀的地。
⑤ 寥廓：旷远、广阔之太空。
⑥ 俨：庄重貌，此为形容词使动用法。

水的性质含有天空的性质，那就是说天空必然含有水的性质。百步以外，镜子上仍能照见人，而人却看不到镜子中的影像，这就是一个验证。于是可知，在虚无的世界，一切都是存在的，在光芒万丈之下，一切东西都是可以看到的。可是世上的人仅知道心中敬仰广阔天空，而不知道走到虚无和空旷之中。虚无之境可以存在于任何地方，神明也离我们很近。因此，有学问有道德修养的人经常保持心志端正，经常庄重而严肃。就可以在广阔空间中邀游，与神明结交而没有灾祸。

Chapter 13

Drifting Clouds

The clouds floating in the sky have no base color, so all kinds of colors can rest on them and leave their colors on them; the bright mirror has not a single stain on it, so it can show the image of all things in the world as it is. When it is said that the nature of water contains the nature of the sky, it means that the sky must contain the nature of water. This can be proven by the fact that at a distance of more than a hundred paces, a person can still be seen in the mirror, but he cannot see the image in the mirror. Everything exists in the world of nothingness, and everything is visible when the thousands of rays of light are shining on it. The average person only admires the vast sky in his heart, but he does not know the importance of stepping into the realm of nothingness. In fact, the realm of nothingness can exist anywhere, and the gods are very close to people. Therefore, the learned and morally cultivated person always keeps a neutral mind, and always stays solemn and serious. In this way, one can roam in the vast universe in this world of nothingness, and befriends the gods without causing calamity.

化书之 **14**

·原文·

哕① 咽

　　有言臭腐之状，则辄有所哕；闻珍羞②之名，则妄有所咽。臭腐了然虚，珍羞必然无，而哕不能止，咽不能已。有惧菽酱③若蠋蛴④者，有爱鲍鱼⑤若凤膏⑥者。知此理者，可以齐奢俭，外荣辱，黜是非，忘祸福。

·白话·

哕 咽

　　当说起恶臭腐烂东西的时候，人们立即呕吐；当听到山珍海味美食的时候，人们在想象刺激下馋得咽口水。在说恶臭腐烂东西的时候，这些东西对人们来说当然是虚假的，听到山珍海味美食的时候，这些东西也肯定是没有的，然而人们还是控制不住自己的呕吐或咽口水。有的人害怕豆酱食物就像害怕天牛幼虫一样，有的人喜爱腌制的咸鱼就像喜爱极其珍贵的凤鸟油脂精华一样。明白这个道理的人，就可

---

①哕：呕吐

②羞：美食

③菽酱：用豆做的酱；

④蠋蛴：桑牛，天牛的幼虫。色白而长。

⑤鲍鱼：腌鱼，味道腥臭。

⑥凤膏：凤的精髓。

以做到将奢华和简朴等同对待，将个人的荣辱置之度外，驱除一切是非，忘却个人祸福。

Chapter 14

Vomiting and Watering

When talking about stinky and rotten things, people immediately vomit; when they hear about great delicacies, their mouths water from imagination. In fact, when talking about stinky and rotten things, these things do not exist around them, and when hearing about delicacies, certainly, none of these things exists either. However, people still can't control their mouths from vomiting or watering. Similarly, some people are afraid of Shu sauce[①] as if they were Qiuqi[②] (worms), while some people love salted fish as if they were the grease of phoenixes[③]. Those who understand this truth can treat luxury and simplicity equally, put aside personal honor and disgrace, drive away grudge and grievance, and forget personal fortune and misfortune.

---

①Shu sauce: It refers to sauces made from beans; Shu is a general term for beans in ancient China.

②Qiuqi: The larvae of longnicorn, which is a type of worm that is long and soft and white in color.

③The grease of phoenixes: Here it denotes some food that is expensive and favored by people.

化书之 15

·原文·

大　化

　　虚化神，神化气，气化形，形化精，精化顾盼，而顾盼化揖让，揖让化升降，升降化尊卑，尊卑化分别，分别化冠冕①，冠冕化车辂②，车辂化宫室，宫室化掖卫③，掖卫化燕享④，燕享化奢荡，奢荡化聚敛，聚敛化欺罔，欺罔化刑戮，刑戮化悖乱，悖乱化甲兵，甲兵化争夺，争夺化败亡。其来也势不可遏，其去也力不可拔。是以大人⑤以道德游泳⑥之，以仁义渔猎⑦之，以刑礼笼罩之，盖保其国家而护其富贵也。故道德有所不实，仁义有所不至，刑礼有所不足，是教民为奸诈，使民为淫邪，化民为悖逆，驱民为盗贼。上昏昏然不知其弊，下恍恍然不知其病，其何以救之哉！

---

① 冠冕：在此处指官位等的差异。

② 车辂：古代帝王为了显示威仪，五级车辂制度。

③ 掖卫：宫廷侍卫。

④ 燕享：又作"宴享"，以酒食招待宾客。古代帝王饮宴群臣。

⑤ 大人：居官在位的人。

⑥ 游泳：浸润。

⑦ 渔猎：窃取。

·白话·

大 化

从虚无中衍化出来意识，从意识中衍化出来生命元气，从生命元气中衍化出来形体，从形体中产生出来思维，思维中产生了向周围环境的关注，从关注中衍化出来与他人相见时候的礼节，从礼节中分别出来褒奖和贬低，褒奖和贬低衍生出来地位高低的尊卑差别，尊卑差别中衍生出来社会等级划分，社会等级划分衍化出来冠冕王侯统治阶层和平民奴隶阶层，冠冕王侯阶层为显示威仪衍生出来车辂制度，为了与车辂制度相应又产生了达官显贵阶层的高墙大院府邸，为了高墙大院的安全需要又衍生出来防卫，在防卫系统保护下产生了聚会饮宴，聚会饮宴发展成为奢侈放荡，奢侈放荡需要聚敛钱财，聚敛钱财过程中为谋取私利产生出来对上面的欺骗蒙蔽，为防治欺骗蒙蔽衍生出来各种刑罚，刑罚的实施又引发出来社会动荡和叛乱，为了平叛又衍生出来军队，军队是权力的支柱，于是又衍生出来争权夺利，争权夺利衍生出来失败灭亡。这样的衍化来势汹汹不可阻挡，衍化的继续发展也无法挽留。于是道德高深之人用道德来浸润它，用仁义来窃取它，用刑罚和礼制来覆盖它，尽力使这种衍化停留在有利于统治者的阶段，用以保护国家和统治阶层的富贵。因此，道德也有虚假的地方，仁义也有达不到的地方，刑罚和礼制也有不足的地方，这些不足，是在教百姓学会奸诈，诱导百姓邪恶和淫荡，促使百姓产生犯上作乱，驱赶百姓成为盗贼。高层统治者稀里糊涂不知道其中弊端，低层统治者懵懵懂懂不知道哪里不正常，这样如何能够解决问题呢。

Chapter **15**

Great Transformation

From nothingness derives consciousness; from consciousness derives Qi; from Qi of life derives form of entities; from form of entities derives thinking; from thinking derives the attention to the surroundings; from the attention to the surroundings derives the etiquette; from the etiquette derive the praise and debasement; from praise and debasement derives the status of the difference between the superior and the inferior; from the difference between the superior and inferior derives the social hierarchy; from the social hierarchy derive the prestigious crowns[①], from the prestigious crowns derives the chariot system[②]; from the chariot system derives the gorgeous mansion of the noble class; from the gorgeous mansion of the prestigious class derives the need for security and the guards; from the need for security and guards derive parties and banquets; from parties and banquets derives lavish debauchery; from lavish debauchery derives the need to collect money from the inferior class to gain personal wealth; from the process of collecting money derives deception to the superior officials; from the need to prevent deception derives various penalties; from the implementation of of various penalties derive social unrest and rebellion; from the need to quell the rebellion derives the army; from the army derives the struggle for power; from the struggle for power derive failure and demise. This series of derivation is unavoidable, and the development of it is unstoppable.

So people with high morality infiltrated it with morality, stole it with benevolence and righteousness, covered it with punishment and rituals, and tried their best to keep this derivation at a stage favorable to the rulers, so as to protect the country and the wealth of the ruling class. Therefore, there are also places where morality is fake, where benevolence and righteousness fail to reach, and where penalties and ritual systems are inadequate. These inadequacies are teaching the people to learn treachery, inducing them to be wicked

---

①Crowns: It is used here to refer to the differences in the ranks of officials.

②Chariot System: It refers order to show the prestige,the ancient emperors designed five different levels of chariots to show different ranks of the officials.

and lascivious, prompting them to commit crimes and driving them to become thieves. How can the problem be solved when the higher rulers are confused and do not know what are the evils, and the lower rulers are ignorant and do not know what is abnormal.

化书之 **16**

· 原文 ·

正　一①

世人皆知苋蓲②可以剖龟，而不知朱草③可以剖人。小人由是知神可以分，气可以泮④，形可以散。散而为万，不谓之有馀；聚而为一，不谓之不足。若狂风飘发，魂魄梦飞；履齿断蚓，首尾皆动。夫何故？太虚⑤，一虚也；太神⑥，一神也；太气⑦，一气也；太形⑧，一形也。命之则四，根之则一。守之不得，舍之不失，是谓正一。

· 白话 ·

正　一

一般人都知道乌龟吃了一种叫做苋蓲的草以后可以化为一群乌龟，但是大家都不知道，人吃了一种叫做朱草的草以后可以将人的意识分割成多个意识。于是我知

---

① 所谓"正一"，即道教中纯正的"一"，"一"在道教之中为世界万物之本，永恒不变。"一"，无处不在，无时不存。万事万物都有"一"，它不召自来，舍之不去，祷之则灵，感之则应，这就是所谓的"正一"。

② 苋蓲：苋，菜名，一年生草木，叶卵圆形。茎细长，种类颇多，茎叶可食，也可以做药；蓲，枯草。

③ 朱草：一种红色的草，可以用作染料。

④ 泮：溶解、分离、散开。

⑤ 太虚：即宇宙天空。

⑥ 太神：此处意为众多神明。

⑦ 太气：此处泛指一切气体。

⑧ 太形：此处指众多有形实体。

道，意识可以分割，元气可以消融，形体也可以消散。神、气、形分散为成千上万份，也不能说分的太多了；成千上万的意识、元气聚集成一个形体，也不能说这一个形体不够用。像狂风吹动长发随风飘舞，像魂魄在梦里任意飞翔；像被木屐踩断的蚯蚓，首尾两段都在动弹。什么原因呢？渺无边际的虚空，就是一个虚空；众多神明，也不过就是一个神；无边无际的生命元气，也不过就是一个元气；大到极端的形体，也不过就是一个形体而已。虚无、意识、元气、形体，名字则是四个，但是根源则只是一个东西。这个东西想守也不能守住，想丢弃也没有办法丢掉，这就是所谓的正一。

Chapter 16

Zheng Yi[①]

People generally know that a turtle can transform into a group of turtles after eating a grass called Xian Zu[②], but no one knows that a human being can divide his consciousness into multiple consciousnesses after eating a type of grass called vermilion grass. Thus, I get to know that consciousness could be divided, Yuanqi could be dissolved, and forms could also be dissipated. Even if consciousness, Yuanqi and forms are dispersed into thousands of parts, one cannot say that there are surpluses; even if thousands of consciousness, Yuanqi and forms are gathered into one, one cannot say that it is not enough. Like the blowing long

---

[①]Zheng Yi refers to the pure "one wholeness" in Taoism, and "one wholeness" is the essence of everything in the world, which is eternal and unchanging.The Zheng Yi (one wholeness) is everywhere, and it exists all the time. All things have this nature, which comes without calling, does not go away even if you desert it. If one prays for it, it will answer the prayers. If one feels it, it will respond.This is the so-called "Zheng Yi".

[②]Xian Zu: It is like amaranth and crispus. Amaranth: a type of herb with oval-shaped leaves. Its stems are slender, and the stems and leaves are edible and can also be used as medicine; Crispus, dry grass.

hair with the wild wind, like a soul flying at will in a dream; like an earthworm broken by clogs, the first and last segments of them are moving. What is the reason? The infinitely void is just one void; the numerous gods are just one god; the boundless Yuanqi is just one Yuanqi; the forms seem so large but it is just one form. Nothingness, consciousness, Yuanqi and forms, on the other hand, have four names, but the root is only one same thing. This thing cannot be guarded even if one wants to, and there is no way to throw it away even if one wants to, and this is what is called Zheng Yi.

化书之 **17**

·原文·

天 地

天地盗太虚①生，人虫②盗天地生，营虹③者，肠中之虫也，搏④我精气，灼我魂魄，盗我滋味，而有其生。有以见我之必死，所以知天之必颓。天其颓乎，我将安有；我其死乎，营虹将安守？所谓奸臣盗国，国破则家亡；蠹⑤虫蚀木，木尽则蠹死。是以大人录⑥精气，藏魂魄，薄滋味，禁嗜欲，外富贵。虽天地老而我不倾，营虹死而我长生，奸臣去而国太平。

·白话·

天 地

天地盗窃太虚之气而生，人类盗窃天地之气而生，营虹盗窃人身中之气而生。而营虹这种虫子，是人肚子里的虫子，这种虫子，夺取我身体里的精气，灼烤我的魂魄，依靠我对食物的滋味而生存。从以前生死更替的事情可以预见我的身体死亡

---

① 太虚：即宇宙天空。
② 人虫：人类和虫豸，此指人。
③ 营虹：寄生虫名。
④ 搏：攫取，窃取。
⑤ 蠹：蛀虫。
⑥ 录：收集。

是必然的，所以知道天地也会有灭亡的时候。天地灭亡了我还能存在吗？我死了，营虹还能活下去吗？这样的事情正像奸臣危害国家，国家破灭了，家庭就没有办法生存了；蛀虫蚀害木头，木头被蚀完的时候，蛀虫的死期也就到了。因此道德高深的人采取自己的精气，深藏自己的魂魄，不去热衷美食滋味，控制自己的嗜好和欲望，将富贵置之度外。这样虽然天地灭亡而我不会死，肚子里的营虹死去而我却能长生不老，就像奸臣伏诛而国家享有太平。

Chapter 17

Heaven and Earth

Heaven and earth are created by absorbing Qi from the universe, and man is created absorbing Qi from heaven and earth. Yingding[1], which is a type of parasite in the belly of man, takes the essence from my body, burns my soul, and depends on my taste for food to survive. I can foresee from the cycle of life and death that death of my body is inevitable, and heaven and earth will also perish. Will I still exist after heaven and earth perish? If I die, will Yingding still live? This is a metaphor. It is like a traitor endangering the state, when the state is destroyed, there is no way for the family to survive; a moth eats the wood, when the wood is completely eaten, the moth's time of death will come. Therefore, a moral person takes his own essence, hides his soul, doesn't go for food or taste, controls desires, and puts wealth out of his mind. If I live in this way, although heaven and earth will perish, I will not die, and the parasite in my stomach will die, but I will live forever, just as a traitor is put to death and the country enjoys peace.

---

[1] Yingding: A type of parasite.

·原文·

稚 子①

稚子弄②影，不知为影所弄；狂夫③侮像，不知为像所侮。化④家者不知为家所化，化国者不知为国所化，化天下者不知为天下所化。三皇⑤，有道者也，不知其道化为五帝⑥之德。五帝，有德者

---

①稚子：小孩子。

②弄：戏弄、玩弄。

③狂夫：骄傲、狂傲的人。

④化：改变。

⑤三皇：说法不一。一般指伏羲、神农、燧人。

伏羲——中华民族人文始祖。所处时代约为新石器时代早期，相传为中国医药鼻祖之一。

伏羲是我国古籍中记载的最早的王。出生在甘肃省的天水陇南一带。伏羲根据天地万物的变化，发明创造了八卦，成了中国古文字的发端，也结束了"结绳纪事"的历史。他又结绳为网，用来捕鸟打猎，并教会了人们渔猎的方法，发明了瑟，创作了《驾辨》曲子，他的活动，标志着中华文明的起始。

神农——传说他发明制作木耒、木耜，教会人民农业生产，遍尝百草，发现药材，教会人民医治疾病。还制定了历法，开创九井相连的水利灌溉技术等。因为他发明农耕技术而号神农氏。

燧人氏，旧石器时代燧明国（今河南商丘）人。《尚书大传》等古籍增补"三皇五帝"中被列为"三皇"之首，奉为"天皇"，尊称"燧皇"。

燧人氏在商丘发明钻木取火，成为中国古代人工取火的发明者，教人熟食，结束了远古人类茹毛饮血的历史，使人类与禽兽的生活习性区别开来，开创了华夏文明，被后世奉为"火祖"。燧人氏生伏羲氏、女娲氏。

⑥五帝：其说不一。一般指黄帝、颛顼、帝喾、尧、舜。

黄帝——轩辕黄帝是中国古史传说时期最早的宗祖神，华夏族形成后被公认为全族的始祖。上古时期约在姬水一带（即渭水—湟水之间）。黄帝族后裔中的一支进入今山西南部，创造了夏文化，遂称夏族。夏族进入中原建立了中国第一个王朝夏代。经过夏、周两代与其他各族的冲突、交往与融合，到战国时期形成了统一的华夏族。

颛顼（zhuān xū）——五帝中第二位帝王，黄帝的孙子，居于帝丘（今河南省濮阳附近）。统治的地区北到现在的河北省一带，南到南岭以南，西到现在的甘肃一带，东到东海中的一些岛屿。

帝喾（dì kù）——五帝中第三位帝王，黄帝之曾孙。与颛顼一起奠定华夏基根，是华夏民族的共同人文始祖。

唐尧——五帝中第四位帝王，因封于唐县，故称唐尧。约公元前2377年出生，15岁时受封为唐侯。20岁时其兄挚为形势所迫让位于他，成为我国原始社会末期的部落联盟长。即位后封其兄挚于唐地为唐侯，并在唐县伏城一带建第一个都城。后因水患西迁，定都山西临汾。唐尧在帝位70年，90岁时禅让于舜，118岁时去世。

虞舜（yú shùn）——五帝中第五位帝王，今山东诸城市万家庄乡诸冯村人。四部落联盟首领，受尧的禅让而称帝。其国号为"有虞"，故称"有虞氏帝舜"。

也，不知其德化为三王之仁义。三王[1]，有仁义者也，不知其仁义化为秦汉之战争。醉者负醉，疥者疗疥，其势弥颠，其病弥笃[2]，而无反者也。

·白话·

稚　子

　　小孩子在玩弄自己的影子的时候，不知道自己也在被影子所玩弄；狂妄自大的人在欺辱镜子里的影像时候，不知道自己也被影像所欺辱。企图教化家庭的人不知道自己也在被家庭教化，企图改变国家的人不知道自己也在被国家所改变，企图改变天下的人不知道也在被天下所改变。三皇为道德高深的圣人，不知道到了五帝时代，自己的奉行的大道已经已经转变成为高尚品行。五帝为品行高尚之人，不知道到了夏禹、商汤、周武王三王时代，自己的高尚品行转变成为仁爱与正义。三王为有仁爱与正义的人，不知道到了秦汉时代，自己的仁爱与正义转变成为战争。醉酒的人还在沉溺醉乡之中，身体上长有疥疮的人还在忙于治疗自己的疥疮，醉的人愈来愈醉，病的人病情越来越严重，是不可能好起来了。

①三王：夏禹、商汤、周文王。或谓禹、汤、文王与武王。
②笃：程度深。

Chapter **18**

Kids

When a kid plays with his shadow and seems to be teasing it, he does not know that he is also being teased by the shadow; when an arrogant person teases the image in the mirror, he does not know that he is also being teased by the image. He who attempts to change his family does not know that he too is being changed by his family; he who attempts to change his country does not know that he too is being changed by his country; he who attempts to change the world does not know that he too is being changed by the world.The Three Clan-rulers (Three Huang)[1], being sages with great morals, did not know that by the time of the Five Emperors[2], their own practices of the great morals would have been transformed into noble characters. The Five Emperors, being men with noble characters, did not know that by the time of the Three Kings[3] — Xia Yu, Shang Tang and Zhou Wu, their noble characters would have been transformed into benevolence and justice. The Three Kings were men of benevolence and justice, did not know that by the time of the Qin and Han dynasties, their benevolence and justice would have been transformed into war. Those who are drunk are still indulging in drunkenness, and those who have scabies on their bodies are still busy treating their scabies, and it is impossible for those who are drunk to get better as they will get even more drunk and for those who are sick to be healed as their illness will be more serious.

---

[1] The three clan-rulers (Three Huang) are the rulers of three clans, and they are Suiren Clan, Fuxi Clan and Shennong Clan respectively. Suiren Clan [Fire clan] are said to have invented the technique of creating fire from flint stones.Fuxi Clan[Fisherman clan] are said to have invented the fish net for fishing, and Shennong Clan [Farmers clan] are said to have invented agriculture and farming.

The 3 clan-rulers were said to appear around 5000—2500 BC, during the neolithic period. At that time, it was still a matriachal society (female-ruled society).

By around 2500 BC, Chinese society turned into a patriarchal society from which came the legendary myths of the Five Emperors.

[2] The Five Emperors (Five Di) are Huangdi (Yellow Emperor), Zhuanxu 5 emperor's (grandson of Yellow Emperor), Diku (great grandson of Yellow Emperor), Yao, or Tang Yao, Shun, or Yu Shun. After the Five Emperors' period, the next ruler came to be known as Yu, who was the founder of Xia dynasty (2100 BC—1600 BC). During the Five Emperors' period there existed an abdication and succession system whereby the alliance chieftain's position was passed on to the most capable person (known as the "Shanrang system"), instead of his sons or any family members.

[3] Three Kings: There are two accounts about who are the Three Kings. One includes Xia Yu, ShangTang, and King Wen of Zhou Dynasty. The other includes Yu, Tang, King Wen of Zhou Dynasty, and King Wu of Zhou Dynasty. They are all kings of Ancient China.

化书之 19

·原文·

阳 燧[①]

　　阳燧召火，方诸[②]召水，感激之道，斯不远矣。高视者强，低视者贼；斜视者狡，平视者仁；张视者怒，细视者佞；远视者智，近视者拙；外视者昏，内视者明。是故载我者身，用我者神，用神合真，可以长存。

·白话·

阳 燧

　　阳燧聚集太阳之火，方诸凝聚露水，这样的事情就接近了感受和反馈的本质。眼睛总是向高处看的人强健，眼睛向低处看的人邪气，眼睛斜视的人诡诈，眼睛平视的人仁义，张大眼睛看东西的人易怒，眯起眼睛看东西的人奸佞；向远处看的人智慧，向近处看的人笨拙；向外看的人昏庸，向身体内部看的人明智。因此，像车船载货一样负载我的，是我的身体，像使用工具一样使用我的，是我的意识。用我的意识与我的身体相合，就可以长存于世。

①阳燧：古时用铜质制成的凹面镜。用以聚集日光，点燃艾炷施灸。
②方诸：月下承露取水的器具

Chapter 19

Yangsui[①]

Yangsui gathers the fire of the sun, Fangchu[②] gathers the dew, and such things approach the essence of feelings and feedback. People can be judged by their eyes. People who always look upward are often strong;people who always look downward are often evil; people who always watch things slantingly are often deceitful; people who always look at things flatly are often benevolent; people who always look at things with their eyes wide open are often irritable; people who always look at things squintedly are often treacherous; people who always look far away are often wise, people who always look near are often clumsy; people who always look outward are often muddleheaded; those who always look within are often wise. Therefore, it is my body that loads me like a cart or a ship carrying cargo, and it is my consciousness that uses me like a tool. If my consciousness is in harmony with my body, I can live long in the world.

---

①Yangsui is a bronze specimen made of copper or copper alloy. When it is facing the sun, the light is first directed to the concave surface and then reflected from different angles. The ancient people use it to gather the sunlight and make fire for acupuncture.

②Fangchu is an apparatus that in ancient times, it was used to gather dew under the moon.

·原文·

死　生

虚化神，神化气，气化血，血化形，形化婴，婴化童，童化少，少化壮，壮化老，老化死。死复化为虚，虚复化为神，神复化为气，气复化为物。化化不间，由环之无穷。夫万物非欲生，不得不生；万物非欲死，不得不死。达此理者虚而乳之，神可以不化，形可以不生。

·白话·

死　生

虚无中产生意识，意识催生出来生命元气，生命元气转化产生血液，血液培育出形体，形体形成婴儿，婴儿成长为儿童，儿童成长为少年，少年成长为壮年，壮年成为老年，老年最终死亡。死亡后又归于虚无，虚无又产生意识，意识又产生生命元气，元气又形成新的形体。这样的变化从无间断，循环往复乃至于无穷。世界万物并非自己想要生出来，但是身不由己，不得不生；世界万物并非自己想要死亡，但是不得不死亡。懂得这个道理并能够与虚无合一，并以这个道理润养自己，意识就可以不再发生变化，形体就可以不形成。

Chapter 20

Life and Death

Consciousness arises from nothingness; consciousness generates Yuanqi of life; Yuanqi of life transforms into blood; blood cultivates forms; forms nurture babies; babies grow into children; children grow into adolescents; adolescents grow into adulthood; adulthood gradually comes to old age; and old age eventually dies. After death, it returns to nothingness, which in turn generates consciousness, which in turn generates Yuanqi, which in turn forms a new form. Such transformations never stop, and the cycle goes on and on to infinity. All things in the world do not want to be born, but they have to be born; all things in the world do not want to die, but they have to die. Knowing this truth and being able to unite with nothingness and nourish oneself with this truth, consciousness can cease to change and forms can stop being formed.

化书之 **21**

·原文·

爪　发①

爪发者，我之形。何爪可割而无害，发可截而无痛？盖荣卫②所不至也。则是我本无害而筋骨为之害，我本无痛而血肉为之痛。所以知喜怒非我作，哀乐非我动，我为形所昧，形为我所爱。达此理者，可以出生死之外。

·白话·

爪　发

指甲和头发，是我的身体的组成部分，但是为什么剪掉指甲对我没有什么伤害，剪掉头发也不会感到疼痛？原因在于身体血液的循环和元气的周流达不到这里。对我本来没有什么伤害的却对我的筋骨有伤害，对我本来没有什么疼痛的但是对我的血肉是疼痛的。因此我知道欢喜或愤怒并非是由我发作出来的，悲哀或高兴也并非是由我引动的，我被我的形体所蒙蔽，我的形体受到我的珍视。懂得这个道理并遵从这个道理去做的人，就可以脱出生死之外了。

---

① 爪发：即指甲和毛发。
② 荣卫：中医学名词。荣指血的循环，卫指气的周流。荣气行于脉中，属阴；卫气行于脉外，属阳。

Chapter 21

Nails and Hair

My nails and hair are part of my body, but why does cutting off my nails not hurt me and cutting off my hair does not cause pain? The reason is that Rong Wei[1] (Yin and Yang) do not reach here. What is not harmful to me is harmful to my muscles and bones, and what is not painful to me is painful to my flesh and blood. Therefore I get to know that joy or anger does not come out of me, nor is sorrow or joy induced by me; I am blinded by my form, and I value my form greatly. He who knows this and follows this truth is free from life and death.

---

[1] Rong Wei: A term used in Chinese medicine. Rong refers to the circulation of blood, and Wei refers to the circulation of Qi. Rong travels in the veins and is Yin; Wei travels outside the veins and is Yang.

·原文·

神　道

太上①者，虚无之神也；天地者，阴阳之神也；人虫者，血肉之神也。其同者神，其异者形。是故形不灵而气灵，语不灵而声灵，觉不灵而梦灵，生不灵而死灵。水至清而结冰不清，神至明而结形不明。水泮②返清，形散返明。能知真死者，可以游太上之京③。

·白话·

神　道

太上，就是虚无的神明；天地，就是阴阳的神明；人，就是血肉之体的神明。他们相同的地方，都是神明，他们不同的地方，就是形体。因此，形体不灵验而生命元气灵验，说的话语不灵验而声音灵验，知觉不灵验而梦境灵验，生命不灵验而死亡灵验。水体即使清澈透亮到极点，结冰后也就不再那么清澈透亮了，神明使清明到极点，有了具体的形体后就不再那么清明了。冰消融后又回归为水的时候，就

①道教最高最尊之神的名前常冠以"太上"二字，以示尊崇。

②泮：溶解，分散。

③太上之京：即所谓玉京。《魏书·释老志》："道家之原，出于老子，其自言也，先天地生，以资万类。上处玉京，为神王之宗；下在紫微，为飞仙之主。"道家称为三十二帝之都，在无为之天。

会重新变得清澈透亮，形体消散以后，意识就会重新回归清明。能够明白死亡真正意义的人，就可以不受形体制约，意识漫游于至高无上的的地方。

Chapter 22

The Tao of God

Tai Shang[1] is a word that refers to the gods of nothingness, heaven and earth are gods of Yin and Yang, and men are the gods of flesh and blood. What they have in common is that they are all gods, and their difference is in their forms. Therefore, the form is not spiritual but the life is spiritual; the words spoken are not spiritual but the voice is spiritual; the perception is not spiritual but the dream is spiritual; the living is not spiritual but the death is spiritual. Even if the body of water is clear and translucent to the extreme, it is no longer so clear and translucent after it becomes ice, and even if the gods are clear and translucent to the extreme, they are no longer so clear after they own a concrete form. When the ice melts and returns to water, it becomes clear again, and after the form dissipates, the gods return to clarity. Those who can understand the true meaning of death can be free from the constraints of form, and their consciousness will roam in the supreme place.

---

[1] The name of the highest and most revered deity in Taoism is often preceded by the word "Taishang" in order to show reverence.

化书之 **23**

·原文·

神 交①

　　牝牡②之道，龟龟相顾，神交也；鹤鹤相唳③，气交也。盖由情爱相接，所以神气可交也。是故大人④大其道以合天地，廓其心以符至真，融其气以生万物，和其神以接兆民。我心熙熙⑤，民心怡怡。心怡怡⑥兮不知其所思，形惚惚⑦兮不知其所为。若一气之和合，若一神之混同，若一声之哀乐，若一形之穷通。安用旌旗，安用金鼓，安用赏罚，安用行伍？斯可以将天下之兵，灭天下之敌。是谓神交之道也。

·白话·

神 交

　　动物之间的雌雄和合的方式，就像乌龟与乌龟之间相互吸引是通过意识进行交

---

①神交：神交即是与神明交合。

②牝牡：雌雄两性。

③唳：鹤鸣声。

④大人：居官在位的人。

⑤熙熙：温和欢乐貌。

⑥怡怡：和顺貌。

⑦惚惚：隐约不清貌。

流的，也像白鹤与白鹤之间相互吸引是通过鸣叫进行生命元气交流的。这都是由于相互之间情爱相投，所以意识和生命元气可以交流。因此道德高深之人将自己的行为合乎天地运行规律，空阔自己的心胸与虚无相符，生命元气融入意识有利生长万物，意识内敛便于与百姓混合为一体。心地平和静宜，不去做任何事情；百姓心里安适自得，不在意自己所处的地方和状态。心里安适自得，什么也不去想，形体轻盈飘忽不知道自己在做什么。就像是所有的元气融合为一种元气，就像是所有的意识混合成一个意识，就像是所有喜怒哀乐的声音都成为了一种声音，就像是所有的阻隔与通畅都集中到一个形体上。不需要用旌旗召唤，不需要用鼓声催促，不需要用奖赏与刑罚，也不需要用军队，就可以用天下所有可以使用的力量为军队，去消灭天下所有的敌人。这就是所说的神交之道。

Chapter 23

Divine Intercourse

The ways animals mate are different. Turtles and tortoises are attracted to each other through the communication of consciousness, and white cranes are attracted to each other through the communication of Yuanqi by chirping. This is all due to mutual love and affection, so that consciousness and Yuanqi can communicate. Therefore, a person with great morality will behave in accordance with the laws of heaven and earth, open his heart and mind to be in line with nothingness, and Yuanqi is integrated into the consciousness to facilitate the growth of all things, and the consciousness is converged to facilitate mixing with the people as one. The heart is in calm and quiet and is not willing to do anything; the people are at ease in their hearts and do not care about the place and state they are in. The mind is at peace, not thinking about anything, and the form is light and floating, not knowing what they are doing. It is like all the Yuanqi is fused into one whole Yuanqi; like all the consciousness mixed into one consciousness; like all the joy, anger, sadness and sound have become one sound; like all the blockage and flux are concentrated into one form. Without summoning with flags, without urging with drums, without rewards and punishments, and without an army, the emperors can use all the power available in the world as an army to destroy all the enemies in the world. This is the way of the divine intercourse that is spoken of.

化书之 **24**

·原文·

大 含

虚化神，神化气，气化形，形气相乘而成声。耳非听声也，而声自投之；谷非应响也，而响自满之。耳，小窍也；谷，大窍也。山泽，小谷也；天地，大谷也。一窍鸣，万窍皆鸣；一谷闻，万谷皆闻。声导气，气导神，神导虚；虚含神，神含气，气含声。声气形相导相含，虽秋蚊之翾翾①，苍蝇之营营②，无所不至也。由此知之，虽丝毫之虑，必有所察；虽啾噤③之言，必有所闻。唯大人之机，天地莫能见，阴阳莫能知，鬼神莫能窥。夫何故？道德仁义之所为。

·白话·

大 含

虚无中产生意识，意识衍化产生生命元气，生命元气衍化养育出形体，形体与元气相互叠加产生声音。耳朵并非要听声音，而声音自己投入到耳朵中来；山谷并

---

① 翾翾：形容飞舞。
② 营营：象声词。指苍蝇嗡嗡的声音。
③ 啾噤：象声词，此处指细声说话的声音。

非要回应声响，而响声自己充满整个山谷。耳朵是小窍，山谷是大窍。山川河流是小窍，天地是大窍。一个窍发出声响，万千个窍都会有声响；一个山谷听到声响，万千山谷都听到声响。声音传导了元气，元气传导了意识，意识传导了虚无；反过来虚无中包含意识，意识中包含元气，元气中包含声音。声音、元气、形体相互传导和包含，尽管秋天蚊子的嗡嗡声音和苍蝇的营营声音很小，却仍然可以传达到每一个角落。由此可知，即使是一丝一毫的微小计谋，也必然会被别人察觉到，即使是很细微很隐秘的言语，也必然会被别人听到。只有道德高尚的圣人，其心机即使天地也无法预见，穷尽阴阳也不能知道，鬼神也无法窥得。这原因何在呢？无他，道德仁义所致。

Chapter 24

Great Inclusion

Consciousness, which arises from nothingness, generates Yuanqi; Yuanqi nurtures and nourishes forms. Forms and energy superimpose each other to produce sound. The ear is not meant to hear sound, but sound itself is put into the ear. The valley is not meant to respond to sound, but the sound itself fills the whole valley. The ear is a small hole and the valley is a big hole. The mountains, rivers and streams are small holes, but the heaven and earth are big holes. When one hole makes a sound, all the thousands of holes echo. When a sound is heard in a valley, the sound can be heard in all the thousands of valleys. Sound conducts Yuanqi, which conducts consciousness, and consciousness conducts nothingness in turn. Conversely, nothingness contains consciousness, consciousness contains Yuanqi, and Yuanqi contains sound. Sound, Yuanqi, and forms conduct and contain each other. Even though the buzzing sound of a mosquito or a fly in autumn is small, it can still reach

every corner. From this, we can infer that no matter how small a scheme is, it is bound to be perceived by others, and no matter how subtle and private the whispers are, they are bound to be heard by others.

Only the mind of the sage with great morality cannot be foreseen even by heaven and earth, cannot be glimpsed by ghosts and gods, and cannot be known even if one exhausts Yin and Yang. What is the reason? Nothing else, it is the power of morality and benevolence.

卷二
Volume 2

术　化

The Transformation of Arts

化书之 **25**

云 龙①

云龙风虎②，得神气之道者也。神由母也，气由子也，以神召气，以母召子，孰敢不至也？夫荡秽者，必召五帝之气，苟召不至，秽何以荡？伏虺③者，必役五星④之精，苟役不至，虺何以伏？小人由是知阴阳可以作，风云可以会，山陵可以拔，江海可以覆。然召之于外，不如守之于内，然后用之于外，则无所不可。

· 白话 ·

云 龙

　　腾云的龙，驭风的虎，它们是得到了精神和元气大道的神物。精神就像是母亲，元气就像是孩子，以精神来召唤元气，就像母亲召唤孩子一样，怎敢不来呢？因此，若要扫荡污秽的，必要召唤来五帝的真气，不然的话，污秽如何才能被涤荡呢？若要降服毒蛇巨蟒，必要役使五星的精华，若是五星的精华不到，怎能降服毒蛇巨

---

①云龙：即是指龙。
②风虎：即是指虎。
③虺（huǐ）：指一种毒蛇。
④五星：是指水星、金星、火星、木星和土星。这五颗星最初分别叫辰星、太白、荧惑、岁星、镇星，这也是古代对这五颗星的通常叫法。

蟒？于是我知道了，阴阳可以改变，风云可以变换，山陵可以拔起，江海可以覆盖。然而从外面召唤而来的，不如将气势养成在体内，然后需要的时候再放出，就没有什么做不到的了。

Chapter 25

The Soaring Dragon

The soaring dragon and tiger are divine creatures that have been given the spirit and Yuanqi. The spirit is like a mother, and Yuanqi is like a child. To summon Yuanqi with the spirit is like a mother summoning her child, so how dare it not come? Therefore, if you want to sweep away the defilement, it is necessary to summon the Qi of the Five Emperors, otherwise, how can the defilement be cleansed? If you want to subdue the poisonous snake, you need to enlist the essence of the Five Stars[1], if the essence of the Five Stars is not available, how can you subdue the poisonous snake? So I can infer that Yin and Yang can be changed, the wind and clouds can be transformed, mountains and hills can be pulled up, and rivers and seas can be covered. However, instead of summoning Yuanqi from the outside, one had better grow and nurture Yuanqi in the body, and then release it when needed. If this can be achieved, there is nothing that cannot be done.

---

[1]Five Stars: It means Mercury, Venus, Mars, Jupiter, and Saturn. They were originally called Chen Xing, Tai Bai, Ying Huo, Sui Xing, Zhen Xing respectively.

化书之 **26**

·原文·

猛　虎

　　猛虎行，草木偃①；毒鸩②怒，土石揭。威之所烁，气之所搏，顽嚚③为之作。小人由是知铗④可使之飞，山河可使之移，万物可使之相随。夫神全则威大，精全则气雄。万惑不能溺，万物可以役。是故一人所以能敌万人者，非弓刀之技，盖威之至也；一人所以能悦万人者，非言笑之惠，盖和之至也。

·白话·

猛　虎

　　猛虎疾行的时候，旁边的草木都趴下了；毒鸩发怒的时候，周围的地面和石头都产生裂痕。那使人惧怕的力量的爆发，附着霸道的气势，就连最顽固和愚蠢的也为之惊惧。于是我知道，我可以使利剑飞舞，使山脉河流移动改道，使世界万物与我相伴。意识越强大，势力就越强大，体内的精气就越充足，气势就越雄大。世间

---

① 偃：倒下。

② 鸩（zhèn）：传说中的猛禽，比鹰大，鸣声大而凄厉。其羽毛有剧毒，用它的羽毛在酒中浸一下，酒就成了鸩酒，毒性很大，几乎不可解救。

③ 嚚（yín）：愚蠢而顽固）。

④ 铗：剑。

万种诱惑也不能使我沉溺其中，世界万物却都可以为我所使役。因此，一个人之所以能敌上万敌人，并非他的武器有多厉害，而是他的威势施加到敌人身上，就会使敌人产生畏惧；一个人之所以能受到万众爱戴，并非是他的言谈笑语感动众人，而是他的平和的气质感染众人，使众人感到亲切。

Chapter **26**

Ferocious Tiger

When the ferocious tiger moves fast, the grass and trees next to it bend down; when the poisonous Zhen[①] gets angry, the ground and rocks around it crack. The outburst of the power with the overbearing aura makes even the most stubborn and foolish afraid. Then I get to know that I could make sharp swords fly, mountains and rivers move and change their course, and all things in the world become my companions.

The stronger the consciousness is, the stronger the might will be; the more abundant the Qi in the body is, the more majestic the aura will be. Even ten thousand temptations cannot make me indulge in them, and all things in the world can be made to serve me. Therefore, it is not the power of one's weapon that makes a person so powerful against ten thousand enemies, but the power and aura shown to their enemies that make the enemies fear; it is not a person's words and laughter that move the people, but his calm temperament that touches the people and makes them feel affectionate.

---

①Zhen: A fierce animal that look like an eagle. Its sound is loud and mournful. Its feathers are highly poisonous, and when its feathers are dipped in wine, the wine becomes hemlock, which is very poisonous and there is no antidote for it.

化书之27

·原文·

用　神

　　虫之无足：蛇能屈曲，蛭①能掬蹙②，蜗牛能蓄缩。小人所以见其机，由是得其师，可以坐致万里而不驰。是故足行者有所不达，翼飞者有所不至，目视者有所不见，耳听者有所不闻。夫何故？彼知形而不知神，此知神而不知形。以形用神则亡，以神用形则康。

·白话·

用　神

　　没有脚爪的虫子可以行走：蛇能屈曲身体，水蛭能蜷缩，蜗牛能隐藏。由此，我窥到其中的奥秘，并由此得到了启发，可以坐着而行万里路程。因此，对在地上行走的来说，有些地方是到达不到的；对在天上飞行的来说，有些地方是去不了；对用眼睛看的，有的东西是看不到的；对用耳朵听的，有些声音是听不到的。这是什么原因呢？因为他们只知道形体的作用，却不知意识的作用，而我，知道意识的作用而不知道形体的作用。用形体来控制意识的必然会败亡，而用意识控制形体的则必然会安康。

---

　　①蛭：水蛭，环节动物，居池沼或水田中，吸食人畜血液。

　　②掬蹙：卷缩。

Chapter 27

The Use of Consciousness

Worms, though without feet or claws, can "walk"; snakes can bend forward; leeches[1] can curl; and snails can contract. I, therefore, peek into the mysteries of these and get inspired by it, and I can travel a million miles while sitting still. For those who walk on the ground, there are places that they cannot reach. For those who fly in the the sky, there are also places that they cannot reach. For those with the eyes to see, there are things that cannot be seen, and for those with the ears to hear, there are also sounds that cannot be heard. What is the reason? Because they only know the role of forms but not the role of consciousness.On the contrary, I know the role of consciousness and yet not the role of forms. He who uses form to control consciousness will suffer defeat, and he who uses consciousness to control form will gain well-being.

---

[1]Leeches: Leeches are annelids, which live in ponds and marshes or paddy fields and suck the blood of humans and animals.

化书之 **28**

水 窦

水窦[①]可以下溺，杵糠[②]可以疗噎。斯物也，始制于人，又复用于人。法本无祖，术本无状，师之于心，得之于象。阳为阴所伏，男为女所制，刚为柔所克，智为愚所得。以是用之，则钟鼓可以使之哑，车毂可以使之斗，妻子可以使之改易，君臣可以使之离合。万物本虚，万法本无，得虚之窍者，知法术之要乎！

水 窦

孔道可以宣泄积水，杵糠可以治疗哽噎。这些东西，都是人制造出来的，又为人所用。道法本来就没有初始，道术本来就没有形状。心中以它为效仿的榜样，而得到的是它表现出来的现象。阳被阴降服，男人被女人控制，刚强的被柔弱的克制，机智过人的被大智若愚的人使用。像这样的使用，则可以使钟鼓暗哑无声，可以使车毂相互碰撞，可以使妻子改嫁他人，可以使君臣之间亲近或厌恶。世界上的万物本来就是虚无的，世界上的千万种道法本来就是什么也没有，能够得知虚无的关键

①水窦（shuǐ dòu）：水道；水之出入孔道。
②杵糠（chǔ kāng）：舂谷杵头上粘着的糠末。可入药。

之处的，也就知道了法术的关键。

Chapter 28

The Sewer System

The channel or sewer system can vent accumulated water, Chu Kang[1] can cure choking. These things are made by people and used by people. In the beginning, Tao has no origin, and Taoism has no shapes. People take it in their heart as an example to follow, but what they get is only the phenomenon it manifests. Yang is subdued by Yin, men are controlled by women, the strong are restrained by the soft, and the witty are used by the wise and foolish. When things run like this, they can make bells and drums dull and silent, chariots and hubs collide with each other, wives remarry others, and emperors and ministers become close or averse to each other. All things in the world are originally from nothingness, and the millions of schools of Taoism in the world are originally from nothingness. Those who grasp the key to nothingness will also grasp the key to the Taoism.

---

[1]Chu Kang: It refers to the chaffs that stick on the bottom of the instrument that is used to smash the grain, which is said to be able to cure choking.

化书之 **29**

· 原文 ·

魍 魉

魍魉①附巫祭言祸福事，每来则饮食言语皆神，每去则饮食言语皆人。不知魍魉附巫祭也，不知巫祭之附魍魉也。小人由是知心可以交②，气可以易，神可以夺，魄可以录③。形为神之宫，神为形之容。以是论之，何所不可？

· 白话 ·

魍 魉

做祭祀的时候，魍魉附身于巫祭身上，借巫祭之口，预言将要发生的祸福之事。每次附身到巫祭身上时，说话和饮食时和食用的食物都像神，而与常人不同，而到了将要离开巫祭身体的时候，说出的话语和食用的食物与常人无异。不知道是魍魉附在巫祭身上，还是巫祭附在魍魉身上。由此，我可知，心可以交出去由他人控制，生命元气可以与他人交换，意识可以被他人夺取，魂魄可以为他人所用。形体是意识的居住之所，意识被形体所容纳。由此推论，还有什么是不可能的呢？

---

① 魍魉（wǎng liǎng）：古代传说中的山川精怪；鬼怪。

② 交：交托出去。

③ 录：录用、采用。

Chapter 29

Mountain Monsters

When the mountain monsters possess the body of the witches in the process of the religious rituals, they prophesy the upcoming fortune and misfortunes through the mouths of the witches. Whenever the monsters possess the body of the witches, they speak and eat like gods, but when they leave the body of the witches, the witches speak and eat like normal people. I do not know whether the mountain monsters are attached to the witches or the witches are attached to the mountain monsters. From this, I can see that the heart can be handed over to others and be controlled by others, Yuanqi can be exchanged with others, the consciousness can be taken by others, and the soul can be used by others. The form is the dwelling place of the consciousness, and the consciousness is contained by the form. Deducing from this, what else is not possible?

---

①Mountain monsters: The legendary monsters in ancient China that live in mountains,.

化书之 30

·原文·

虚 无

鬼之神可以御，龙之变可以役，蛇虺可以不能螫，戈矛可以不能击。唯无心者火不能烧，水不能溺，兵刃不能加，天命不能死。其何故？志于乐者犹忘饥，志于忧者犹忘痛，志于虚无者可以忘生死。

·白话·

虚 无

可以抵御鬼的精神，可以驾驭龙的变化，可以使蛇蝎毒虫无法螫人，可以使戈矛武器无法攻击人。唯独心无旁骛、摆脱了世俗影响的人，就算烈火也无法焚烧他的身体，洪水也无法使其溺亡，刀兵之祸不能将其加害，就算达到常人的死亡年龄，依然可以保持不死之身。这是什么原因呢？全身心快乐的人，他就会忘记饥饿。终日只是忧愁的人就会忘掉自己身上的疼痛，全心全意的投入到虚无中的人就会忘掉自己的生死。

Nothingness

The spirit of a ghost can be defended, the change of a dragon can be controlled, a poisonous serpent can be made unable to bite people, and a spear or a weapon can be made unable to attack people. Only a man whose heart is peaceful and free from worldly influences cannot be engulfed by fire, cannot be drowned by floods, and cannot be harmed by the scourge of the sword, and he can remain immortal after he has reached the normal age of death. What is the reason? He who is all filled with happiness will forget his hunger. He who is immersed with sadness will forget the pain in his body, and he who devotes himself wholeheartedly to nothingness will forget his life and death.

化书之 **31**

·原文·

虚 实

方咫①之木置于地之上，使人蹈②之而有馀。方尺之木置于竿之端，使人踞③之而不足。非物有小大，盖心有虚实。是故冒大暑而挠者愈热，受灸灼而惧者愈痛。人无常心，物无常性。小人由是知水可使不湿，火可使不燥。

·白话·

虚 实

一尺见方的木板放置在地面上，人踩踏在木板上会觉得地空间挺富足；而当把这块木板置于高高的竿子顶端的时候，即便坐着不动，也会让人觉得地方太小了。这并非是由于木板的尺寸变了，而是人的心理发生了从踏实到心虚的变化。因此，原本心里就烦躁的人，在暑天里更会感到天气比实际的气温更热，心里对火焰害怕的人，在受到火焰灼伤时，会比常人觉得更疼痛。人的心不是永远不变的，物体的特性也不是永远不变的。据此，我可以得知，有可以使水无法湿润，使火无法燥热的方法。

---

① 表示1尺见方。尺是我国传统的长度计量单位，十寸为一尺。现代三尺约等于1 m。每平尺等于1108.89平方厘米。
② 蹈：踩踏。
③ 踞：蹲，坐。

Grounded or Unsettled

When a square-Chi[①] board is placed on the ground, a person steping on it will feel that there still remains plenty of room; when the board is placed on top of a tall pole, even when sitting still on it, the person will feel that there is too little room left. This is not a change in the size of the plank, but a change in the mental state of the person who is either grounded or unsettled. Thus, a person who is originally irritable will feel hotter than it really is in the heat of the day, and a person who is afraid of fire will feel more pain when he is burned by it. The heart of a man does not remain the same forever, nor do the properties of objects. I learn from this that there are ways to keep water from being moist and fire from being hot and dry.

[①] Chi and Cun are the traditional unit of length measurement in China. 10 Cun equals 1 Chi, and 3 Chi equals 1 meter. Here, 1 square Chi is 1108.89 square centimeters.

化书之 **32**

狐　狸

狐狸之怪，雀鼠之魅①，不能幻明镜之鉴者，明镜无心之故也。是以虚空无心而无所不知，昊天②无心万象③自驰，行师无状而敌不敢欺，大人无虑而元精自归，能师于无者，无所不之。

狐　狸

狐狸所表现出来的鬼怪，老鼠和鸟雀表现出来的蛊惑，之所以在明镜面前无法隐藏，无所遁形，皆因为明镜没有心。虚空也是没有心的，所以能无所不知；苍天也是没有心的，所以万物按照自然的规律自行运动；顺应天地之和而动的军队，打仗没有固定的方式、方法，所以敌人不敢轻视招惹；道德高深的人，心中没有任何的思虑，而生命精气自行回归体内。能够效法并做到虚无的人，便可无所不能。

---

① 魅：蛊惑、迷惑。

② 昊天：苍天，辽阔广大的天空。

③ 万象：一切事物、一切景象。

Chapter 32

The Fox

The weirdness shown by the fox and the evilness shown by the mouse and the bird can all be revealed clearly before the mirror because the mirror has no heart. Nothingness has no heart, therefore it knows everything. The universe has no heart, therefore, everything goes on in accordance with the law of nature. An army that fights in a war in tune with the harmony of heaven and earth will never be taken lightly by their enemies because they have no fixed means of fighting. A person who has high standards of morality is always in a carefree state and has nothing in his heart to worry about, so that Yuanqi returns to his body. He who is able to follow the example of nothingness and achieve nothingness is omnipotent.

化书之 33

转 舟

转万斛①之舟者，由一寻②之木；发千钧③之弩④者，由一寸之机⑤。一目可以观大天，一人可以君兆民。太虚⑥茫茫而有涯，太上浩浩而有象。得天地之纲，知阴阳之房，见精神之藏，则数可以夺，命可以活，天地可以反覆⑦。

转 舟

能使得巨大的舟船转动方向的东西，不过是八尺大小的木头，发射有千钧之力的强大弩箭的东西，由一寸大小的扳机所控制。一只眼睛就可以观察到整个天空，一个人可以统治天下百姓。即使最大的虚空茫茫渺渺其实也有边际，即使是至高无上的东西浩浩荡荡其实也有形状。如果能够掌握提契天地的关键及要领，懂得阴阳

---

①斛：中国旧量器名，亦是容量单位，古代以十斗为一斛。

②寻：古代长度单位。八尺为一寻。

③钧：古代重量单位。三十斤为一钧。四钧为一石。

④弩：用机械发射的弓，也叫窝弓，力强可以及远。其种类很多，大的要用脚踏，或用腰开，有数矢并发者称连弩。

⑤机：弩机，弓上发箭的装置。

⑥太虚：宇宙天空。

⑦返覆：翻覆，倾动。"返"同"反"。

之所在，窥见精神藏匿的地方，则可以控制天运，可以掌握自己的性命，可以将天地颠倒过来。

Chapter 33

Reverse the Direction of a Boat

The thing that could make a huge boat that weighs thousands of Hu[①] reverse its direction is nothing more than a piece of 8-Chi[②]-sized wood; a powerful crossbow with the force of a thousand Jun[③] is fired by a 1-Cun[④]-sized trigger. One eye could observe the whole sky, and one man could rule the people of the world. Even Tai Xu[⑤] actually has borders, and even Tai Shang actually has a shape. If one can master the essentials of heaven and earth, know where Yin and Yang are, and glimpse where the spirit hides, one can control the fortunes of heaven, master one's life, and turn heaven and earth upside down.

---

①Hu: In ancient China, Hu and Dou are both the names of measuring instruments and units of capacity. 10 Dou equals one Hu and 1 Dou equals 6 KG.

②Chi: Chi is a Chinese length measurement. 1 Chi equals 13.12335958 inches.

③Jun: Unit of weight in Ancient China. 1 Jun equals 15kg.

④Cun: Cun and Chi are all Chinese length measurements. 1 Cun equals 1.312335958 inches.

⑤Tai Xu: The great universe.

化书之 **34**

心 变

　　至淫者化为妇人①，至暴者化为猛虎，心之所变，不得不变。是故乐者其形和，喜者其形逸，怒者其形刚，忧者其形戚。斯亦变化之道也。小人由是知顾六尺之躯，可以为龙蛇，可以为金石②，可以为草木。大哉斯言！

心 变

　　极端荒淫的男子最后变成了女人，极端暴虐的人最后变成了猛虎。心性变了，形体也不得不变。因此，高兴的人，其容貌一团和气；喜悦的人；其容貌舒适安逸；愤怒的人，其容貌刚直；忧愁的人，其容貌悲伤。这就是变化之道。因此，我知道，若我专注于六尺之躯，可以使它变成龙蛇，也可以使它变成金属或石块，还可以使他们变成草木。这的确是至理名言呀。

---

①至淫者化为妇人：《汉书五行志第七下之上》："哀帝建平中，豫章有男子化成女子，嫁为人妇，生一子。长安陈凤言此阳变为阴，将亡继嗣。"
②金石：泛指自然界中的各种金属和石块。

Chapter **34**

The Change of Heart

Men whose sexual lust comes to the extreme finally become women, and those whose rage burns to the extreme finally become tigers. When the heart changes, the form also has to change. Therefore, a happy person looks peaceful, a joyful person looks relaxed, an angry person looks rigid, and a sad person looks desolate. This is also the way of change. So I realize that when my consciousness is focused on my six-Chi body, I can become a dragon or a snake, a piece of metal or a stone, and a blade of grass or a tree. This is indeed the true wisdom.

化书之 **35**

珠 玉

悲则雨泪，辛则雨涕；愤则结瘿[①]，怒则结疽[②]。心之所欲，气之所属，无所不育。邪苟为此，正必为彼。是以大人节悲辛，诚愤怒；得灏气[③]之门，所以收其根；知元神之囊，所以韬[④]其光；若蚌内守，若石内藏，所以为珠玉之房。

珠 玉

人悲痛的时候便会泪如雨下，受到辛辣刺激的时候，便会涕泪长流；易生气的人，脖子上会长出瘤子，常暴怒的人，身上会长出毒疮。心里的欲望，都会聚集相应的气，这种气就会培育出相应的东西。邪气是一种样子，正气必然是相反的。于是道德高深之人节制自己的悲痛情绪，不去嗜好辛辣滋味食物，时时刻刻告诫自己以防范愤怒之心；获知浩然正气的大门所在，所以将元气收根归源；知道元神之所在，所以处世低调，隐藏声名才华；犹如蚌蛤默默守护体内的珍珠，又如玉璞小心

---

① 瘿：病理学指机体组织受病原刺激后，局部细胞增生，形成的囊状性赘生物。
② 疽：中医指一种毒疮
③ 灏气：正大刚直之气。
④ 韬：隐藏，隐蔽

翼翼珍藏内部的宝玉，所以蚌蛤和玉璞才能成为珍珠和宝玉隐藏之处。

Chapter 35

Pearl and Jade

Tears fall like rain when one is grieving; snot and tears flow long when one is stimulated by pungency; a person who is easily angered grows a tumor on his neck, and a person who is often furious grows poisonous sores on his body. Any desire that the heart wants to express will gather the corresponding Qi, and this Qi will cultivate the corresponding things. Whatever the evil Qi generates, the righteous Qi will bring out the opposite. So a person of great moral character restrains himself from grief, does not eat spicy food, and guards against anger; he knows how to gain righteousness, so he returns Yuanqi to its source; he knows where Yuanqi is, so he keeps a low profile in the world and hides his reputation and talent; he is like a clam silently guarding the pearl in his body, and an uncut jade carefully hiding the precious jade inside, so the clam and the uncut jade can become the hidden place of the pearl and precious jade.

化书之 **36**

蠮 螉①

夫蠮螉之虫，孕螟蛉②之子，传其情，交其精，混其气，和其神。随物大小，俱得其真。蠢动无定情，万物无定形。小人由是知马可使之飞，鱼可使之驰，土木偶可使之有知，婴兒似乳母，斯道不远矣。

·白话·

蠮 螉

有一种叫蠮螉的虫子，它们将螟蛉的幼虫当做自己的孩子来哺育，将自己的秉性传给它，用自己的生命精气与它交融，用自己的元气与它们的元气融合，用自己的元神与它糅合。虽然这些螟蛉幼虫形体大小各有不同，但是都得到了蠮螉的真髓。动物没有一成不变的秉性，世上万物也没有永恒不变的形体。于是，我们推知，可以让马飞起来，可以让鱼在地上奔跑，可以让泥人木偶有智慧，可以让婴儿变成哺乳他的妈妈的模样。这样就接近道的本质了。

---

① 蠮螉（yē wēng），即蜾蠃（guǒ luǒ），寄生蜂，捕螟蛉（míng líng）并在其身上产卵。蠮螉幼虫出生后以螟蛉为食物。古人误以为蠮螉不产子，喂养螟蛉幼虫为自己的孩子。
② 螟蛉，桑虫。

Yeweng[①]

There is a kind of insect called Yeweng, which nurse the the larvae of Mingling[②] as own children, passing their own nature to them, mingling with them with their own life essence, mixing with them their own Yuanqi, blending with them with their own spirit. Although the larvae of these Mingling are of different sizes, they have all received the true essence of Yeweng. The nature of animals is not unchangeable, and the form of everything in the world is changeable. So it can be deduced that we can make a horse fly, a fish run on the ground, a clay puppet have intelligence, and a baby take the form of its mother. In this way one approaches the essence of Tao.

---

①Yeweng: Or Guoluo, are parasitic wasps that catch Mingling(a type of moth) and lay eggs on them. The larvae of Yeweng feed on Mingling. The ancient people mistakenly thought that Yeweng did not lay eggs and fed the larvae of Mingling as their own children.

②Mingling: A type of bollworm.

化书之 **37**

· 原文 ·

胡 夫①

胡夫而越②妇，其子髯③面而矬④足；蛮⑤夫而羌⑥妇，其子拗⑦鼻而昂首。梨接桃而本强者其实毛，梅接杏而本强者其实甘。以阴孕阳，以柔孕刚，以曲孕直，以短孕长，以大孕小，以圆孕方，以水孕火，以丹孕黄。小人由是知可以为金石，可以为珠玉，可以为异类，可以为怪状，造化之道也。

· 白话 ·

胡 夫

西域男人娶越国女子为妻，他们的孩子满面胡须，个子矮小，脚大；西域男人娶羌族女子为妻，他们的孩子有鹰钩鼻子，昂首。在桃树上嫁接梨，由于桃树为本体，遗传优势强，结出来的果实上面就有桃毛；在杏树上嫁接梅子，由于杏树为本

---

①胡：我国古代泛称北方边地与西域的民族为胡。

②越：古时江浙粤闽之地越族所居，谓之百越。"越"通"粤"。

③髯：古称多须者为髯。

④矬：身短曰矬。

⑤蛮：古代对南方少数民族的泛称。

⑥羌：我国古代西部民族之一。

⑦拗：弯曲。

体，遗传优势强，结出来的果实就有杏子的甘甜。凭借阴，可以孕育阳；凭借柔，可以孕育刚强；凭借弯曲，可以孕育着正直；凭借短，可以孕育长；凭借大，可以孕育小；凭借圆，可以孕育方；凭借水，可以孕育火；凭借红，可以孕育黄。我于是知道，可以变化为金石，可以变化为珠玉，可以变化为禽兽鬼怪，可以变化为奇形怪状，这就是造化之道。

Chapter 37

Husband of Hu[①]

If a man from Hu marries a woman of Yue[②], their sons will be bearded, short and have large feet; If a man of Hu marries a woman of Qiang[③], their children will have aquiline noses and their heads will always keep a up-tilted position. The pear that is grafted on a peach tree will have fuzz on it due to the strong genetic advantage of the peach tree. The plum that is grafted on an apricot tree will have the sweetness of the apricot due to the strong genetic advantage of the apricot tree. Yin breeds Yang, softness breeds strength, bending breeds straightness, shortness breeds length, largeness breeds smallness, roundness breeds squareness, water breeds fire, and red breeds yellow. I then get to know that everything can change into gold or stone, into pearls or jade, into birds or animals, into beasts or ghosts, or into other strange forms, and this is the Tao of creation.

①Hu: In ancient China, the ethnic groups of the northern borderlands and western regions are referred to as Hu.

②Yue: An ethnic group in ancient China, the Yue people lived in Jiangsu, Zhejiang, Guangdong and Fujian.

③Qiang: One of the ancient western ethnic groups in China.

·原文·

阴 阳

阴阳相搏，不根而生芝菌；燥湿相育，不母而生蠰蛴①。是故世人体阴阳而根之，学燥湿而母之，无不济者。小人由是知陶炼五行②，火之道也；流行无穷，水之道也；八卦③环转，天地之道也；神物乃生，变化之道也。是以君子体物而知身，体身而知道。夫大人之道幽且微，则不知其孰是孰非。

·白话·

阴 阳

阴气和阳气相互竞争，没有根茎却可以生长出灵芝蘑菇来；干燥和潮湿相互孕育，没有母体却能育生出毒虫来。因此人们体悟阴阳，并以阴阳调和为根本，模仿干燥和潮湿相互孕育，悉心养育，没有不成功的。我于是知道，陶冶锻炼金木火水土五行是火的大道，江河的川流不息是水的大道，八卦循环转动，是天地运行的大道。神奇灵

① 蠰蛴：桑牛，天牛的幼虫。色白而长。
② 五行：水、火、木、金、土，道教指构成各种物质的五种元素。
③ 八卦：八卦是中国道家文化的深奥概念，是一套用三组阴阳组成的形而上学的哲学符号。其深邃的哲理解释自然、社会现象。八卦：乾qián、坤kūn、震zhèn、巽xùn、坎kǎn、离lí、艮gèn、兑duì。这八个卦象，在不同的方面，代表不同的事物。比如：在宇宙观上：乾为天，坤为地，震为雷，巽为风，坎为水，离为火，艮为山，兑为泽。另外，在家庭观、动物观、身体观、运动观及权力观等方面代表其他不同的事物。

异的事物出生是自然变化的大道。于是有学问有修养的人通过对他物的体验而了解自己身体内部运行规律，通过对自己身体内部运行规律的体悟而懂得了道的本性。德行高尚、志趣高远的人为人处世表现为幽静而且隐匿，于是就无法判断他的是与非。

Chapter 38

Yin and Yang

　　When Yin and Yang compete with each other, Lucid Ganoderma and mushrooms can grow without roots. Dryness and moisture together can breed Qiuqi[1] without a mother. Therefore, people can perceive Yin and Yang and take the harmony of Yin and Yang as the fundamental. What's more, they imitate the mode of dryness and moisture and nurture Yin and Yang painstakingly. I then get to know that the practice and lakes of Wuxing[2] —Metal, Wood, Fire, Water and Earth are the natural law of Fire; the endless flow of rivers is the natural law of water; the cyclic turnover of Bagua[3] of heaven, earth, thunder, wind, water, fire, mountains and lakes is the law of the operation of heaven and earth; and the birth of miraculous and spiritual things is the law of natural change. Thus, the learned and cultivated people perceive the inner workings of their own body through the experience of things, and gets the nature of the Tao through the realization of the inner workings of their own body. A person of great morals and high aspirations behaves quietly and in low-profile in the world, so it is impossible to judge whether he is right or wrong.

---

①Qiuqi: The larvae of longnicorn, a type of worms that are long and soft and white in color.

②Wuxing: It refers to water, fire, wood, metal and earth, which in Taosim is believed to make up various substances.

③Bagua: Bagua is an esoteric concept of Chinese Taoist culture, a set of metaphysical and philosophical symbols composed of three groups of Yin and Yang. Its profound philosophy explains natural and social phenomena. The Eight Diagrams: 乾 qián, 坤 kūn, 震 zhèn, 巽 xùn, 坎 kǎn, 离 lí, 艮 gèn, 兑 duì. These eight diagrams, in different aspects, represent different things. For example, in the cosmic view: Qian for the sky, Kun for the earth, Zhen for thunder, Xun for wind, Kan for water, Li for fire, Gen for mountains, and Dui for lakes. In addition, in the family view, animal view, body view, movement view and power view they represent other different things.

·原文·

海 鱼

海鱼有以虾为目者，人皆笑之。殊不知古人以囊萤为灯者，又不知昼非日之光则不能驰，夜非烛之明则有所欺。观傀儡之假而不自疑，嗟明友之逝而不自悲，贤与愚莫知，唯抱纯白①、养太玄②者，不入其机。

·白话·

海 鱼

海鱼中有一种鱼用虾来当做自己的眼睛，人们都嘲笑它。殊不知古人中也用萤火虫做灯烛的，殊不知白天若是没有太阳的光照，人们就不能驱车出行；夜晚若没有灯烛照明，就什么也看不到。看见假的傀儡却毫不怀疑，叹息朋友的去世而不为自己感到悲哀，贤达和愚昧都不能分辨。唯独心怀纯净，远离俗世、全部精气神用于虚无、韬光养晦的人，才不受蒙蔽。

---

①纯白：纯净无暇，不染一丝红尘。
②太玄：最神妙难捉摸的，最深奥的，虚无。

Sea Fish

There is a kind of fish in the sea that use shrimps as their eyes, and people laugh at them. What people do not know is that the ancient people also used fireflies as candles or lights. People cannot drive if there is no light during the day, and cannot see anything and if there is no light during the night. When people see a false puppet, they never suspect it, and when they see the death of a friend, they feel sad for their friends but not for themselves. They cannot tell foolishness from wisdom. Only one whose heart is pure and whose whole essence is devoted to nothingness will not be deluded.

化书之 **40**

涧 松

涧松所以能凌霜者，藏正气也；美玉所以能犯火者，蓄至精也。是以大人昼运灵旗^①，夜录^②神芝，觉所不觉，思所不思，可以冬御风而不寒，夏御火而不热。故君子藏正气者，可以远鬼神、伏奸佞；蓄至精者，可以福生灵、保富寿。夫何为？多少之故也。

涧 松

水涧中生长的松树之所以能抵抗霜寒，是因为松树内藏有抗寒及再生的生命元气；极品玉石之所以能抵抗烈火，是因为玉石内蓄积有精气。所以，有德高人白天就像挥舞旗帜指挥军队一样指挥着意识，夜晚就像采用灵芝补身体一样采取精气神补充意识，对外界的知觉没有了，思维也停止了，可以在冬天身处风中不感到寒冷，在夏天骄阳下而不感到灼热。因此，有学问有修养的人珍藏自己防御抵抗和再生的生命元气，就可以使鬼神辟易，可以歼灭奸佞邪恶的人；蓄积了形成天地万物的精微物质，就可以造福生灵，保障自己的富贵与长寿。为什么可以这样呢？不过是因为生命元气和精微物质的数量很多而已。

---

① 灵旗：指古代出征，在战旗上画上星宿，举旗出征。此句表示君子白天都在筹划大事情。
② 神芝：指灵芝，指君子夜间采集灵芝，他们一身正气，思考的都是大师。

Chapter 40

Pine Trees

The reason why the pine trees growing in the water stream can resist the frost and cold is that they contain the Yuanqi of resistance to cold and of regeneration; the reason why the finest jade can resist the fire is that the jade accumulates the fine and subtle substances that form all things in heaven and earth.A virtuous person commands his consciousness during the day like waving a flag to command an army, and takes essence to replenish his consciousness at night like adopting Lingzhi to replenish his body; his perception of the outside world is gone, and his thinking stops, and he can be in the wind in winter without feeling cold, and in the fire in summer without feeling hot. Therefore, a learned and cultivated person who treasures his Yuanqi can repel the ghosts, and annihilate the treacherous and evil people. Having accumulated the fine and subtle substances that form all things in heaven and earth, he can benefit all living beings and guarantee his own wealth and longevity. Why is this possible? It is only because the amount of Yuanqi and subtle substances is large.

化书之 41

·原文·

动 静

动静相磨，所以化火也；燥湿相蒸，所以化水也；水火相勃，所以化云也；汤盎投井，所以化雹也；饮水雨日，所以化虹霓也。小人由是知阴阳可以召，五行可以役，天地可以别构，日月可以我作。有闻是言者，必将以为诞。夫民之形也，头圆而足方，上动而下静，五行运于内，二曜明于外。斯亦构之道也。

·白话·

动 静

运动和静止相互摩擦产生火；干燥的空气和湿润的空气相互熏蒸，继而产生水；水和火相互排斥生成云；将盛放着热水的瓦罐投入水井中，会产生冰雹；吸口水背对阳光向空中喷洒水雾，可以形成彩虹。我于是知道，我可以招摄阴阳，可以使役五行，可以改变天地的结构，可以改变日月的运行规律。有的人听到这样的话，必定会认为是荒诞无稽之言。殊不知人的形体头圆而足方，似天圆地方；上半部身体动而下半部身体静，似天空风云变幻而大地沉默无言；五脏运作体内，似天地间五行生生不息的循环；双目列于形体表面，似日月列于天地之外。这也是天地构造的方式呀。

Dynamic and Static

A moving object and a static object rubbing against each other will produce fire; dry air and moist air competing with each other will produce water; water and fire repelling each other will produce clouds; a tile pot with hot water thrown into a well will produce hail; a person who sucks a mouthful of water and sprays the water into the air while standing with his back to the sun will produce a rainbow. I then get to know that I can invoke Yin and Yang, have Wuxing at my command, change the structure of heaven and earth, and alter the movement of the sun and the moon. When hearing such words, people must think that I am absurd and nonsensical. What they do not know is that the form of the body—round head and square foot, is similar to the structure of heaven and earth—the round heaven and the square earth. The upper part of the body moves while the lower part of the body is still, and it is just like that the sky is changing while the earth is static; The five internal organs operate in the body, just like the endless cycle of the Wuxing in heaven and earth; and the eyes are on the surface of the body, just like the sun and the moon are outside of heaven and earth. This is also the way heaven and earth are constructed.

化书之 **42**

·原文·

声 气

操琴瑟之音，则翛①然而闲；奏郑卫之音②，则乐然而逸；碎瓴甓③之音，则背膂④凛森；挝鼓鼙⑤之音，则鸿毛踯躅⑥，其感激之道也如是。以其和也，召阳气，化融风，生万物也。其不和也，作阴气，化厉风，辱万物也。气由声也，声由气也，气动则声发，声发则气振，气振则风行而万物变化也。是以风云可以命，霜雹可以致，凤凰⑦可以歌，熊罴⑧可以舞，神明可以友，用乐之术也甚大。

①翛（xiāo）：无拘无束，自由自在。
②郑卫之音：春秋战国时郑、卫国的俗乐。儒家以《论语·卫灵公》有"郑声淫"之语，后因以郑卫之音通指淫靡的乐歌或文学作品。《礼记·乐记》："郑卫之音，乱世之音也。"
③瓴甓：砖，陶制容器，似瓶。
④膂：脊骨。
⑤挝：敲打，击打；鼓鼙：乐器，大鼓和小鼓，进军时以励战士。
⑥踯躅：住足，踏步不前。
⑦凤凰："凰"，本作"皇"，传说中的鸟名，雄曰凤，雌曰凰。
⑧熊罴：熊和罴。罴为熊的一种，即棕熊，又叫马熊，毛棕褐色，能爬树，会游泳。皆为猛兽。

声 气

听到琴瑟演奏的声音时，心情就会放松，有了闲情逸致，自由自在；演奏春秋战国时郑国和卫国民间音乐时，则感到快乐和舒适；摔破瓶罐，就会被声音惊吓得后脊梁骨冒凉气。军队里擂动战鼓时，受到鼓声激荡，羽毛漂浮在空中的荡来荡去的无法落地。安静平和的声音，可以招摄阳气，可以化为暖融的春风，促进万物生长；凶暴戾气的声音，则招摄阴气，化作凛冽暴风，摧残万物。气的变化是由声音引发的，声音的变化又是由气的变化引发的。气振动就发出了声音，声音发出后又会引起气的振动，气振动产生了风并影响万物随之发生变化。因此，风云变化可以被我指挥，冰霜冰雹可以被我制造出来，凤凰可以为我唱歌，熊罴可以为我跳舞，神仙可以和我做朋友，音乐的作用是巨大的。

Chapter 42

Sound and Qi

When you play the qin and the se[①], the sound will make you relaxed and you will feel at ease; when you play the folk music of the states of Zheng and Wei during the Spring and Autumn Period, you will feel happy and comfortable. However, when you break a jar, you will be freaked out by the breaking sound. When the war drums are beaten in the army, stirred by the drums, the feathers will float around in the air and can not land. Soft and calm

①The qin and the se: Both are Chinese musical instruments of the zither family. The qin has 7 strings while the se has 25-50 strings according to its size.

sounds can attract Yang energy, which can be turned into a warm spring breeze, promoting the growth of all things; on the other hand, violent and hostile sound incurs Yin energy which can be turned into a fierce wind, destroying all things. Changes in Qi are triggered by sound, and changes in sound are triggered by changes in Qi. The vibration of Qi emits sound, which in turn causes the vibration of Qi; the vibration of Qi generates the wind and influences all things to change accordingly. Therefore, the changes of wind and clouds can be directed by me; frost and hail can be created by me;the phoenix can sing for me; the wild beasts can dance for me; the gods can be friends with me. The power of music is huge.

大　同

虚含虚，神含神，气含气，明含明，物含物。达此理者，情可以通，形可以同。同于火者化为火，同于水者化为水，同于日月者化为日月，同于金石者化为金石。唯大人无所不同，无所不化，足可以与虚皇①并驾。

·白话·

大　同

虚无之中含着虚无，意识中含着意识，元气中含着元气，光明中含着光明，万物中又含着万物。如果是可以明白这个道理的，则性情可以相通，形体亦可以相同。与火相同的可以化为火，与水相同的可以化为水，与日月相同的可以化为日月，与金石相同的化为金石。唯有道德高深的人，没有什么是他们不可以同的，也没有什么是不可以化的，因此其成就足可以与虚皇并驾齐驱。

---

① 虚皇：道教神祇名称。又名元始天尊。

Universal Harmony

The nothingness in the form is connected to the nothingness outside the form; the consciousness in the form is connected to the consciousness outside the form; the vital energy in the form is connected to the vital energy outside the form; the brightness in the form is connected to the brightness outside the form; the entity in the form is connected to the entity outside the form. Those who have realized this can share the same temperament and the same form with everything. Those who can be the same with fire can become fire, those who can be the same with water can become water, those who can be the same with the sun and the moon can become the sun and the moon, and those who can be the same with metal and stone can become metal and stone. Only those with high morality can be the same with anything, because they can transform into anything, and their achievements can be on a par with the god of Nothingness[1].

---

[1]The god of Nothingness: The name of a god in Taoism who is also called Heavenly Worthy of the Primordial Beginning.

化书之 44

·原文·

帝　师

镜非求鉴于物，而物自投之；橐[①]非求饱于气，而气自实之。是故鼻以虚受臭，耳以虚受声，目以虚受色，舌以虚受味。所以心同幽冥[②]，则物无不受；神同虚无，则事无不知。是以大人夺其机[③]，藏其微，羽符[④]至怪，阴液[⑤]甚奇，可以守国，可以救时，可以坐[⑥]为帝王之师。

·白话·

帝　师

镜子并非是乞求物体来照镜子，而物体自己将形象投入其中；风箱并非想要用空气填饱肚子，而空气自己进来填满风箱。因此，鼻子由于里面有空虚的地方而闻到气味，耳朵因为里面有空虚的地方而听到声音，眼睛因为里面没有颜色而看到颜色，舌头因为本身没有味道而品尝出味道。所以，心处在幽远玄妙之地，则没有什

①橐：风箱。
②幽冥：即幽冥，暗昧。
③机：玄机。
④羽符：道士的图符。道士巫师所画的一种图形或线条，相传可以役鬼神，辟病邪。道教的一种道符。
⑤阴液：露水。此似指符水，溶有符箓灰烬的水。道士用来治病。
⑥坐：自然地，全不费力地。

么东西不被感觉到；意识虚无，则没有什么事情不知道。因此道德高深的人懂得了空虚是无所不受无所不知的关键，他们可以藏匿自己的微小的缺憾。虽然他们绘制的图符非常怪异，符水异常奇特。但是却可以守卫国家，可以解救时难，也可以成为帝王恭请的老师。

Chapter 44

The Emperor's Teacher

The mirror does not beg the object to look into it, but the object itself puts its image into it; the bellow does not want to fill its belly with air, but the air itself comes in and fills the bellow. Thus the nose smells because there is emptiness in it, the ear hears sound because there is emptiness in it, the eye sees color because there is no color in it, and the tongue tastes because there is no taste in itself. Therefore, when the mind is in a place of profound mystery, there is nothing that cannot be felt; when the consciousness communicates with emptiness, there is nothing that cannot be known. The morally advanced person understands that nothingness is the key to omniscience. They can hide their tiny deficiencies. Although they draw very strange spells and the water thar holds the spell is unusually peculiar, these things can guard the country and save the country in time of difficulties. Naturally, they can become teachers that are respectfully called for by the emperor.

化书之 45

·原文·

琥 珀①

琥珀不能呼腐芥，丹砂②不能入焦金，磁石不能取惫铁③，元气不能发陶炉④。所以大人善用五行之精，善夺万物之灵，食天人之禄，驾风马⑤之荣。其道也在忘其形而求其情。

·白话·

琥 珀

腐烂的草芥，不能被吸附到琥珀当中，朱砂也不能投入进融化的黄金中，磁石来不能吸取生了锈的铁块，陶炉不可能产生生命元气。所以道德高深的人善于使用五行的精华，善于改变万物的灵气，享用神仙的福运，享有驾驭神车的荣誉。其根本在于忘掉了形体而致力于与无形和万物心理相通。

①琥珀：琥珀即松柏树脂的化石。
②丹砂：即朱砂。
③惫铁：生锈的铁块。依文意，惫与"败"同义。
④陶炉：烧制陶器，冶炼金属的盛火器。
⑤风马：神车。

Chapter 45

The Amber

Rotten grass cannot be sucked into the amber; vermilion cannot be put into the melted gold; magnets can not absorb rusted iron; pottery furnace cannot produce Yuanqi of life. So the person with high standards of morality is good at using the essence of the Wuxing to change the aura of all things, enjoy the blessings of the gods and the glory of driving a divine carriage. The fundamental of this lies in forgetting the form and devoting oneself to connecting with the formless and the heart of all things.

卷 三
Volume 3

德 化

The Transformation of the Virtues

化书之 **46**

·原文·

五　常①

　　儒有讲五常之道者，分之为五事②，属之为五行，散之为五色③，化之为五声④，俯之为五岳⑤，仰之为五星⑥，物之为五金⑦，族之为五灵⑧，配之为五味⑨，感之为五情⑩。所以听之者若醯鸡⑪之游太

---

① 五常：仁、义、礼、智、信。

② 五事：指古代统治者修身的五件事，谓貌恭、言从、视明、听聪、思睿。使国致富的五件事。决定战争胜负的五种因素。《尚书·洪范》："敬用五事。"《汉书五行志第七》："五事，一曰貌，二曰言。三曰视，四曰听，五曰思。貌曰恭，言曰从，视曰明，听曰聪，思曰睿。"有五件事，一件是容貌，二件是言谈词章，三件是眼睛的观察力，四件是听辨是非，五件是内心思虑。这五件事，是人类从上天接受的天命，是君王进行治理百姓的条件。君王的容貌是恭谨，恭谨就是敬。畏言谈是顺从，顺从就是可以听从。眼力是明察，明察就是知道贤能和不贤能、能分别好坏。听力是明辨是非，听力敏锐能听到事情并明辨其中的意思。思虑是宽容，宽容是说没有不能容纳的。恭敬可以写作肃敬，顺从可以写作治理，明察可以写作哲智，听察是非可以写作咨询思考，宽容可以写作圣明。恭敬可以写作肃敬，是说君王如果在内心有恭敬的姿态，天下没有不肃敬的。顺从可以写作治，是说君王的言论可以顺从，臣下顺从行事而天下可以太平无事。明察可以写作哲智，哲智就是明智。君王明察贤能就可以被进荐，没有才能的人退出官位，天下人知晓善就鼓励从善，知晓恶就以恶事为耻辱。听力明察可以写作咨询思考，咨询思考就是咨询故事，君王听力明察是非，就会听到事情后和臣下商议，所以事情不能失去谋略。宽容又作圣明，是圣明者设有的，君王心地宽大没有不能容纳的，圣明能施行建树，事情各自得到合适的结果。

③ 五色：黑、黄、赤、白、青五种颜色。

④ 五声：宫、商、角、徵、羽，亦称"五音"。为古乐五声音阶的五个名称。

⑤ 五岳：即中岳嵩山，东岳泰山，西岳华山，南岳衡山，北岳恒山。

⑥ 五星：汉刘向《说苑辨物》以岁星（木）、萤惑（火）、镇星（土）、太白（金）、辰星（水）为五星。

⑦ 五金：《汉书·食货志（上）》："金、刀、龟、贝"注："金谓五色之金也，黄者曰金、白者曰银，赤者曰铜，青者曰铅，黑者曰铁。"后通称金、银、铜、铁、锡为五金。

⑧ 五灵：古代传说的麟、凤、龟、龙、白虎。

⑨ 五味：酸、苦、甘、辛、咸。

⑩ 五情：喜、怒、哀、乐、怨。

⑪ 醯（xī）鸡：喜聚于醋酱上的小飞虫。醯，醋。

虚，如井蛙之浮沧溟①，莫见其鸿濛②之涯，莫测其浩渺之程。日暮途远，无不倒行。殊不知五常之道一也，忘其名则得其理，忘其理则得其情。然后牧之以清静，栖之以杳冥③，使混我神气，符我心灵。若水投水，不分其清；若火投火，不间其明。是谓夺五行之英，盗五常之精，聚之则一芥可包，散之则万机④齐亨。其用事也如酌醴⑤以投器，其应物也如悬镜以鉴形。于是乎变之为万象，化之为万生，通之为阴阳，虚之为神明。所以运帝王之筹策，代天地之权衡⑥，则仲尼其人也。

· 白话 ·

五　常

　　儒家有讲五常之道的，分开来说就是五事，连缀来说就是五行，分散它就成为五色，转化它就成为五声，若俯瞰就是五岳，若仰视就是五星，物化它就是五金，集中它就是五灵，与食物相配就是五味，就情感而言就是五情。所以听到这一说法的人就像微小的蠛虫游荡于虚空，就像井底之蛙漂浮在大海上，无法看见太空边际在哪里，也无法测量大海的遥远里程。眼见太阳要落山了，而路途还很遥远，只能掉头折返。儒者不知道五常之道就是"一"，忘掉它的名字就会得到它的构造和运行规律，忘掉它的构造和运行规律就会得到它的情性。然后用清净来管理它，让它停

---

① 沧溟：指大海。

② 鸿濛：广阔无边。

③ 杳冥：幽暗深远。

④ 万机：万事之机。机，事物变化之所由。《庄子·至乐》："万物皆出于机，皆入于机。"疏："机者，发动，所谓造化也。"

⑤ 酌醴：斟美酒。筹策：古代计算用具。引申为谋画。

⑥ 权衡：称量物体轻重之具。权。称锤；衡，称杆。引申为平正，衡量，法度。

留在渺茫莫测的地方，使它与我的精神气魄相互混合，与我的思想情感相符合。就像把水投入水中，分不出来孰清孰浊；就像将火投入火中，分不出来孰明孰暗。可以说是改变五行的英华，借用五常的精髓，将它们聚集在一起则是一个微小的芥子就可以包容，将它们散布开来，则万种繁杂事务都能通达顺利。用它来做事情就像用斟酒到酒杯里一样顺势而成，用它来回应事情就像用悬挂的镜子来鉴别形象一样让事情的本来面目无所遁形。于是，五常可以变成万千物象，可以转化成万千生灵；五常内相通的为阴阳，将五常置于虚无的为神明。所以运用帝王谋略，代行天地的法度的，就是孔丘这个人了。

Chapter 46

Five Virtues of Confucian Ethnics

In Confucianism, there are Five Virtues[1], which are in fact Five Things[2] when being discussed separately, Wuxing (or five elements) when connected, Five Colors[3] when dispersed, and Five Sounds[4] when transformed. They are Five Mountains[5] if you look down on them, Five Stars[6] if you look up at them. When materialized, they are Five

---

[1]Five Virtues: In Confucius theory, the Five Virtues refer to the virtues of Benevolence, Righteousness, Ritual, Wisdom and Faithfulness.

[2]Five Things: It refers to the five things that the ancient rulers practice in the process of self-cultivation: being respectful in appearance, obedient in speech, clear in sight, intelligent in hearing, and wise in thinking.

[3]Five Colors: It refers to the five colors of black, yellow, red, white, green.

[4]Five Sounds: It refers to the five names of the pentatonic scale of ancient Chinese music.

[5]Five Mountains: It refers to five famous mountains in China—Songshan Mountain, Taishan Mountain, Huashan Mountain, Hengshan Mountain (Hunan) and Hengshan Mountain (Shanxi).

[6]Five Stars: It refers to the stars of Venus, Jupiter, Mercury, Mars, and Saturn.

Metals[1]. When concentrated, they are Five Spirits[2], and Five Emotions[3] when they are emotionalized. When being matched with food, they are Five Tastes[4]. So those who hear it are like tiny midges wandering in the void, like frogs who used to be at the bottom of the well floating on the ocean, unable to see where the edge is, and not knowing how far they have to go to reach the other side through such a vast space. Seeing that the sun is going down, and the road is still far away, everyone would turn around and go back.

What people do not know is that the Five Virtues is actually one unity. Forgetting its name, one will get its construction and laws of operation. Forgetting its construction and laws of operation, one will get its nature. Then I manage it with purity and let it stay in an unpredictable place of insignificance, so that it mixes with my mind and spirits. It is like pouring water into water and not being able to distinguish which is clear and which is muddy; throwing fire into fire and not being able to distinguish which is bright and which is dark. It can be said to take away the essence of the Five Elements and the Five Virtues. When being gathered together, a tiny seed of grass can hold them. When being spread out, they can make everything go smoothly. Utilizing it to do things is like pouring wine into a wine glass, in which the wine just takes the opportunity to follow the trend, and utilizing it to respond to things is like using a hanging mirror to identify the image so that images of things are not hidden. Thus, the Five Virtues can be transformed into thousands of phenomena and life forms. The one that is connected within Five Virtues is Yin and Yang, and the one that puts Five Virtues into nothingness is the gods. So it is Confucius instead of the emperor who makes decisions, and it is Confucius instead of heaven and earth who weighs the pros and cons.

---

[1] Five Metals: It refers to the five metals of gold, silver, copper, iron and tin.

[2] Five Spirits: It refers to the five animals of Kylin (an imaginary animal in Ancient China), Phoenix, Tortoise, Dragon, and White Tiger, and these animals all simbolize good luck.

[3] Five Emotions: It refers to the emotions of joy, anger, sorrow, happiness, and grievance.

[4] Five Tastes: It refers to sourness, bitterness, sweetness, spiciness and saltiness.

化书之 47

·原文·

飞 蛾

天下贤愚，营营然若飞蛾之投夜烛，苍蝇之触晓窗。知往而不知返，知进而不知退。而但知避害而就利，不知聚利而就害。夫贤于人而不贤于身，何贤之谓也？博于物而不博于己，何博之谓也？是以大人利害俱忘，何往不臧？

·白话·

飞 蛾

天下之人，不论贤人还是愚人，都像飞蛾奔向夜间的烛光那样往来盘旋，毕生都在追求名利，又像拂晓时分的苍蝇撞窗户一样到处乱撞。他们只知去而不知道返，只知道进而不知道退；只知躲避危害，追求利益，不知道由于积聚利益而导致危害。衡量别人的贤良程度，却不亲身实施，这算得上什么贤良呢？广博地了解事物，对自己却了解不多，这算什么广博呢？因此道德高深的人把所有的利害都忘掉，还怕去往什么地方不能得到益处吗？

The Moth

People in the world, whether wise or foolish, spend their lives in the pursuit of fame and fortune, like moths fluttering to the candle at night or flies hitting the window at dawn, knowing only to set out but not to return, only to advance but not to retreat; knowing only to avoid harm and to pursue profit, but not knowing that the accumulation of profit leads to harm. What kind of virtuousness is it to measure the virtuousness of others, but not do it yourself? What kind of knowledge is it to know things extensively, but not much about yourself? Therefore, a moral person forgets all the benefits and harms, how could he be afraid of not getting benefits wherever he goes?

化书之 48

· 原文 ·

异 心

虎踞于林，蛇游于泽，非鸱鸢①之仇；鸱鸢从而号之，以其蓄异心之故也。牛牧于田，豕眠于圈，非乌鹊②之驭；乌鹊从而乘之，以其无异心之故也。是故麟有利角，众兽不伏；凤有利觜，众鸟不宾；君有奇智，天下不臣。善驰者终于蹶③，善斗者终于败。有数④则终，有智则穷。巧者为不巧者所使，诈者为不诈者所理。

· 白话 ·

异 心

猛虎盘踞在森林，毒蛇游行在水泽，与天上飞翔的鹰隼并没有什么怨仇，但是在鹰隼随着它们的移动而飞翔时，它们却会发出受到威胁时的吼叫声，是因为鹰隼对它们怀有戒心。在田野吃草的牛，趴在猪圈里睡觉的猪，它们并非是由乌鸦控制的，但是在它们走动时，乌鸦喜鹊却可以站在它们身上而无恙，是因为乌鸦对它们没有异念。因此，尽管麒麟头上有尖利的角而众兽并不服从；尽管凤凰有尖利的喙而众鸟并不归顺；尽管君王有过人的聪明才智而天下并不臣服。善于奔跑的最终总

---

① 鸱鸢（chī yuān）：鹰隼。
② 乌鹊：即乌鸦。
③ 蹶：颠仆，跌倒。
④ 数：数术，古代关于天文、历法、占卜的学问。

会跌倒，善于格斗的人最后总会失败。有学问的人，学问终有用完的时候，有才智就会有才智枯竭的时候。机巧的人被不机巧的人所使用，狡诈的人被不狡诈的人所治理。

Chapter 48

Disloyalty

Tigers sit in the forest, snakes swim in marshes, and they hold no grudge against the flying eagles. However, when the eagles fly after thern, they will screech furiously because they are wary of them. Cows grazing in the fields and pigs sleeping in the pigsty are not controlled by crows, but when they are walking, crows can stand on them without hurting them because the crows are not wary of thern.

Therefore, although the Kylin[①] has sharp horns on its head, the beasts do not obey; although the phoenix has a sharp beak, the birds do not submit; although the emperor has extraordinary wisdom, the world does not bend the knee. People who are good at running will eventually fall down, and those who are good at fighting will end up being losing. If people own knowledge and wit, there will be a time when their knowledge and wit are exhausted. Clever people are used by simple people, and cunning people are governed by people who are not cunning.

---

①Kylin: An imagery animal in ancient China.

化书之 49

·原文·

弓 矢

天子作弓矢威天下，天下盗弓矢以侮天子。君子作礼乐以防小人，小人盗礼乐以僭君子。有国者好聚敛，蓄粟帛、具甲兵以御贼盗，贼盗擅甲兵、踞粟帛以夺其国，或曰："安危德也。"又曰："兴亡数也。"苟德可以恃，何必广粟帛乎？苟数可以凭，何必广甲兵乎？

·白话·

弓 矢

天子制作了弓箭武器用来威慑天下，天下的人就盗取弓箭武器用来反抗天子。高尚的人制定礼节音乐制度用来防御奸佞的人，奸佞的人就盗用礼节音乐制度来获取较高身份地位，反过来压制高尚的人。国家的统治者热衷聚敛钱财，蓄积粮食布匹，置办军队来防贼防盗；贼盗招兵买马，占据粮食布匹来抢夺统治者的国家。有人说"国家的安危取决于统治者的德行"，或者说"国家的兴亡是由天数确定的"。如果可以依靠德行来统治国家，何必要广蓄钱粮呢？如果天数可以作为凭据，何必要穷兵黩武呢？

Chapter **49**

Bows and Arrows

The emperors make the weapons of bows and arrows to intimidate their people, but their people will steal the bows and arrows to rebel against them. The noble man makes a system of social norms and ethics to defend against the treacherous man, but the treacherous man will misappropriate the system to gain a higher status to suppress the noble man. The rulers of the country are keen to gather money, store grain and cloth, and build an army to guard against thieves and burglars, but the thieves and burglars recruit troops and horses and loot the grain and cloth to rob the rulers of the country. It is said that "the security of a country is determined by the virtue of the ruler", or "the rise and fall of a country is determined by its destiny". If a country can be ruled by virtue, why should there be a need to store up money and grain? If the destiny could decide the rise and fall of a country, why do people indulge in arms and weapons?

化书之 **50**

聪　明

无所不能者，有大不能；无所不知者，有大不知，夫忘弓矢然后知射之道，忘策辔^①然后知驭之道，忘弦匏^②然后知乐之道，忘智虑然后知大人之道。是以天下之主，道德出于人；理国之主，仁义出于人；亡国之主，聪明出于人。

·白话·

聪　明

无所不能的人，肯定在某些方面是无能的；无所不知的人，在某些事情上肯定是无知的。忘掉弓箭然后才能体悟到射箭的玄妙，忘掉马鞭马缰然后才能体会到驾车的玄妙，忘掉乐器才能体会到音乐的玄妙，忘掉自己的才智和思虑然后才能领悟到得道之人的玄妙。因此，天下共同尊崇的人，必是道德操行高于众人；善于治理国家的人，必是仁爱和正义高于众人；导致国家灭亡的人，必是自以为是的小聪明高于众人。

---

① 策辔（cè pèi）：马鞭与马缰。泛指驭马的工具。
② 絃匏（xián páo）：弦和匏。均乐器名。古代八音中"匏曰笙，丝曰絃"，因亦泛指乐器。

Intelligence

He who is omnipotent must be powerless in certain things; he who is omniscient must be ignorant in certain things. He who forgets his bow and arrows can realize the subtlety of archery; he who forgets the whip and bridle can realize the subtlety of driving; he who forgets his musical instruments can realize the subtlety of music; he who forgets his own wisdom and thoughts can realize the subtlety of the man who has attained Tao. Therefore, the person who is respected by the whole world must have better moral conduct than others; the person who is good at governing the country must have a better sense of benevolence and justice; the person who causes the downfall of the country must have greater pretentious cleverness and intelligence than others.

·原文·

有 国①

有国之礼，享②郊庙，敬鬼神也；亹③龟策④，占吉凶也。敬鬼神，信祸福之职⑤也；占吉凶，信兴亡之数也。奈何有大不信，穷民之力以为城郭，夺民之食为储蓄？是福可以力取，是祸可以力敌；是疑贰于鬼神，是欺惑于龟策，是不信于天下之人；斯道也，赏不足动，罚不足惧，国不足守。

·白话·

有 国

国家统治者制定的祭祀活动，是建造祭天地的郊宫和祭祖先的宗庙，以表示对鬼神的敬畏；是不停地用龟甲和蓍草占卜测吉凶。敬鬼神是相信祸福都有鬼神司职，占卜测吉凶是相信国家兴亡由天数而定。但为什么有国君根本不信天意，穷尽百姓的人力物力财力建起城郭，抢夺百姓的食物为自己蓄积？他们认为幸福是可以凭着

---

① 有国：拥有国家政权的人，最高统治者。
② 享：祭祀。
③ 亹（wěi）：勤勉不知疲倦。
④ 龟策：古时候常使用龟壳和蓍草来占卜吉凶。
⑤ 职：掌管、执掌。

武力抢夺的，灾祸是可以凭着武力抗拒的。这样是对鬼神猜忌离心，对龟甲欺骗迷惑，是不会被天下人信任的。以这样方式做事情的人，奖赏不足以使人心动，惩罚不足以使人畏惧，他们可以获取国家却守不住国家。

Chapter 51

The Rulers of a Country

The ritual system developed by the rulers of the country includes building palaces in the suburbs for worshiping heaven and earth and ancestral temples to honor demons and gods, and constantly using tortoise shells and herbs in divination. To worship demons and gods is to believe that they are in charge of disasters and blessings. To divine the future is to believe that the rise and fall of a country is determined by destiny. It is a pity that there are rulers who do not believe in demons and gods at all, and they force their people to labor for them and exhaust material resources to build cities and fortresses, and rob their people's food to save up for themselves. They assume that if the divination is a blessing, they can seize it by force; if it is a curse, they can avoid it by force. They are suspicious of the demons and gods and divination, and they are not trusted by anyone in the world. If the rulers of a country do things in this way, people will not be moved by any reward, and will not be intimidated by any punishment. Thus, the rulers can get a country by force, but they will sooner or later lose it.

化书之 **52**

黄 雀

　　黄雀之为物也，日游于庭，日亲于人而常畏人，而人常挠^①之。玄鸟^②之为物也，时游于户，时亲于人而不畏人，而人不挠之，彼行促促^③，此行佯佯^④；彼鸣啾啾^⑤，此鸣锵锵^⑥；彼视矍矍^⑦，此视汪汪^⑧；彼心戚戚，此心堂堂^⑨。是故疑人者为人所疑，防人者为人所防。君子之道，仁与义、中与正，何忧何害！

黄 雀

　　黄雀作为一只禽鸟，白天游荡在庭院之中，天天和人亲近但常常害怕人，而人

---

①挠：抓捕。
②玄鸟：燕子。因其羽毛黑，故名。
③促促：小心谨慎的样子。
④佯佯：同"洋洋"，舒缓貌。得意喜乐貌。
⑤啾啾：象声词。指兽啼鸟鸣声。
⑥锵锵：象声词。指铃声、凤鸣声、乐声。也作"将将"。
⑦矍矍（jué）：惊惶，急视貌，目不正视貌。
⑧汪汪：深广貌。亦用以形容人的气度宽弘。
⑨堂堂：形容容仪庄严大方。君子之道仁与义《周易 说卦》："是以立天之道曰阴与阳，立地之道曰柔与刚，立人之道曰仁与义。"

常常去抓捕它；燕子作为一只禽鸟，时不时的穿堂过户，有时候也与人亲近但从不怕人，而人不去抓捕它。黄雀处处都在拘谨小心，燕子时时都是悠闲自在；黄雀鸣叫起来细声细气，燕子的鸣叫起来声音响亮；黄雀小心翼翼的东张西望，燕子炯炯有神的环顾四周；黄雀忧心忡忡，燕子堂堂正正。因此，怀疑别人的人被别人所怀疑，戒备别人的人被别人所戒备。而君子处事，秉持仁义，保持中正，怎么会有忧愁和畏惧呢？

Chapter **52**

The Siskin

The siskin, as a type of bird, always wanders in the courtyard in the daytime. It's close to people but always afraid of people, and people often tease it. The swallow, as a type of a bird, flies through the hall of people's houses from time to time. It's sometimes also close to people but never afraid of people, and people do not tease it. The siskin is forever restrained and cautious, while the swallow at ease; the siskin always chirps softly, while the swallow cries loudly; the siskin always looks around cautiously, while the swallow looks around fearlessly; the siskin is always worried, while the swallow upright. Thus, those who suspect others are suspected by others, and those who are wary of others are warded off by others. Whereas a gentleman deals with things with benevolence, righteousness and justice, how should he have sorrow or fear?

化书之 **53**

笼 猿

笼中之猿，踊跃万变不能出于笼；匣中之虎，狂怒万变不能出于匣；小人之机，智虑万变不能出于大人之道。夫大人之道，如地之负，如天之垂。无日不怨，无人不欺，怨不我怒，欺不我夷，然后万物知其所归。

笼 猿

被关在笼子中的猿猴，无论怎样翻腾跳跃也无法逃出笼子；关在铁栅栏里的猛虎，无论怎样狂暴怒吼也无法逃出铁栅栏；见识浅陋的人的谋划，竭尽心机千变万化也无法跳出道德高深之人的掌握。道德高深之人的道，就像大地，负载万物，就像天宇，笼罩万物。上天和大地没有一天不遭怨恨，没有哪个人不散罔他们。可是遭到抱怨也不忿怒，受到欺负也不受伤，然后万物才知道自己的宗旨。

Ape in the Cage

An ape in a cage cannot escape from the cage, no matter how much it tumbles and jumps; a tiger in an iron cage cannot escape from the iron cage, no matter how furiously it roars; a shallow person cannot escape from the grasp of a highly moral person, no matter how sophisticated and flexible his plans are. The Tao of the highly moral man is like the heaven and the earth which can hold and envelop everything in this world. They are complained about every day, and bullied by every one. However, they will not get angry even when they are complained about, and cannot be hurt even when they are bullied. Thus, all things know what their purposes are.

化书之 54

· 原文 ·

常　道

仁义者常行之道，行之不得其术，以至于亡国。忠信者常用之道，用之不得其术，以至于获罪。廉洁者常守之道，守之不得其术，以至于暴民。财^①辩者常御之道，御之不得其术，以至于罹祸。盖拙在用于人，巧在用于身。使民亲稼则怨，诚民轻食则怒。夫饵者鱼之嗜，膻者蚁之慕，以饵投鱼鱼必以惧，以膻投蚁蚁必去，由不得化之道。

· 白话 ·

常　道

秉持仁义信念的人按照仁义行事，由于行事的方法不对，以至于导致亡国。秉持忠君诚信信念的人，根据忠信做事，由于做事的方法不对，以至于获罪。秉持廉洁信念的人，做事坚守廉洁，由于坚守的方法不对，以至于引起民怨。才智机辩是公认的妙法，由于驾驭的方法不对，以至于招来横祸。这样的错误是由于将这些用于他人，而正确的是将这些用于自身。强迫百姓去从事农业劳动则招致抱怨，告诫

---

①财：元本作"才"。

百姓要节俭饮食则引起愤怒。鱼饵是鱼儿的嗜好的美味，膻腥的食物是让蚂蚁心仪的美食，但是若把鱼饵投向鱼儿，鱼儿必然畏惧，把膻腥之物扔向蚂蚁，蚂蚁必然四处奔逃，这都是不懂得正确的方法所致。

Chapter 54

Customary Practices

Those who act with benevolence cause the downfall of a country because they act in the wrong way. Those who act with loyalty and integrity get punished because they act in the wrong way. Those who deal with things with integrity, but still provoke public discontent because they deal with things in the wrong way. Those who are intelligent and eloquent finally incur misfortune on themselves because they do it in the wrong way. What they do wrong is that they should not impose these practices on others instead of themselves. Forcing the people to work the land invites complaints, and admonishing them to eat frugally causes anger. For example, fish bait is a delicacy for fish, and foul food for ants, but when fish bait is thrown at them, the fish are bound to get spooked; when foul food is thrown at ants, the ants are bound to run away. This is because people do not know the right way of moral cultivation.

化书之 **55**

[原文]

感 喜

感父之慈，非孝也；喜君之宠，非忠也。感始于不感，喜始于不喜。多感必多怨，多喜必多怒。感喜在心，由①物之有毒，由蓬②之藏火，不可不虑。是以君子之业，爵之不贵，礼之不大，亲之不知，疏之不疑，辱之不得，何感喜之有。

[白话]

感 喜

对父亲的慈爱千恩万谢，并非是孝顺；对君王的宠信欢欣喜悦，并非是忠心。感谢始于不感谢，欢喜始于不欢喜。有很多的感谢必然有很多的怨恨，有很多的欢喜必然有很多的愤怒。感谢和欢喜这些东西在心里，就像物品里面藏有毒药，就像柴火堆里面藏有火种，不能不考虑到。因此道德高深的人为人处事，爵位加身并不感到自己有多么尊贵，受到他人尊敬也不会自高自大，对他人与自己亲近的举动也没有应和，对他人与自己疏远的行为也不去疑虑，他人欺辱自己也不感到是受到欺辱，在心里哪里还会有什么感谢和欢喜呢。

---

① 由：通"犹"。
② 蓬：草名，即蓬蒿。

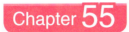

Rejoicing

It is not filial piety to be thankful for a father's kindness; it is not loyalty to rejoice in the favor of an emperor. Thankfulness begins with unthankfulness, and joy begins with unjoyfulness. There must be as much gratitude as resentment, and there must be as much rejoicing as anger. Thankfulness and rejoicing are things in the heart that cannot be disregarded, just as there is poison hidden in things, and kindling hidden in a woodpile. Therefore, a person with great morality does not feel honored by his title, does not feel arrogant when he is highly respected by others, does not blindly follow the actions of others who are close to him, does not have doubts about the actions of others who are distant from him, and does not feel humiliated when others humiliate him, so how could there be gratitude or joy in his heart?

·原文·

太 医①

太医之道，脉②和而实者为君子，生之道也；挠③而浮者为小人，死之道也。太卜④之道，策⑤平而慢⑥者为君子，吉之道也；曲而利⑦者为小人，凶之道也。以是论之，天下之理一也，是故观其国，则知其臣；观其臣，则知其君；观其君，则知其兴亡。臣可以择君而仕，君可以择臣而任。夫揖让可作而躁静不可作，衣冠可诈而形器不可诈，言语可文而声音不可文。

·白话·

太 医

根据医生诊断病情的经验，脉象平和搏动沉实的一般都是有学问有修养的人，是符合养生之道的脉象；脉象杂乱轻浮的一般都是品格低劣狡诈的人，是加速身体

---

①太医：在封建社会，专门为帝王和宫廷官员等服务的医生。

②脉：中医指脉息、脉搏。

③挠：被搅动或阻止。浮：脉象名。

④太卜：太卜，周朝叫大卜，官阶下大夫，掌阴阳卜筮之法，通过卜筮蓍龟，帮助天子决定诸疑，观国家之吉凶。

⑤策：蓍草，用于卜筮，此处代指占卜。

⑥平而慢：即平和舒缓的卦象，为正常的卦象。

⑦曲而利：曲突、变化剧烈的卦象。

衰败死亡的脉象。根据占卜的经验，蓍草摆动缓慢、草叶平直的一般都是有学问有修养的人，是为吉祥的卦象；蓍草摆动急促、草叶弯折的一般都是品格低劣狡诈的人，是为大凶的卦象。据此推论，天下的事情和这样的事情是一样的。因此，观察一下这个国家的情况，就知道这个国家中大臣的情况；观察一下这些大臣的情况，就可以知道这个国家君王的情况；观察一下这个君王，就可以知道这个国家兴亡变化的大概趋势。大臣可以选择自己中意的君王为之效力，君王可以选择自己中意的大臣来任职。礼节可以作假而性情的浮躁与否不能作假，衣冠服饰可以作假而气质形体无法作假，说话的言语可以作假而说话的声音不能作假。

Chapter 56

Royal Doctor

According to the royal doctor's experience in diagnosing people's condition, the pulse that is calm and solid generally indicates that the person is a learned and cultivated, and this type of pulse shows that their bodies are in a good condition. On the contrary, the pulse that is restless and irregular generally indicates a person of evil and cunning character, and this type of pulse shows the decay and death of the body. In divination, when the Grass of Shi[1] swings slowly and the grass blades are straight, it is an auspicious sign which generally indicates a learned and cultivated person. On the contrary, when the Grass of Shi swings rapidly and the grass blades are bent, it is an ominous sign that generally indicates a despicable and cunning person. Everything in the world fits this rule. Therefore,

---

[1] The Grass of Shi is used in ancient divination. It artificially mimics the movement of things we want to predict through the movement of the grass. The law of the movement indicates whether there is fortune or misfortune, which is revealed through hexagrams

by observing and surveying a country, we know how its ministers and officials behave; by observing and surveying the ministers and officials of a country, we can know how the emperor of this country behaves; by observing the emperor, we can know the general trend of the changes of the rise and fall of a country. Ministers can choose their favorite emperors to serve, and emperors can choose their favorite ministers to serve them. The greeting rituals can be faked but not the resflessness of the heart; the clothes and dress can be faked but not the temperament and form; the words of speech can be faked but not the voice.

化书之 **57**

·原文·

谗　语

藏于人者谓之机①，奇于人者谓之谋②。殊不知道德之机，众人所知；仁义之谋，众人所无。是故有赏罚之教则邪道进，有亲疏之分则小人入。夫弃金于市，盗不敢取；询政于朝，谗不敢语，天下之至公也。

·白话·

谗　语

人们把对别人隐藏起来的东西称为机理（事情变化的道理），把出人意料的东西称为谋略。却没想到道德的机理是非是大家都知道的，但是要做事情符合仁义，很多人是做不到的。因此，有了赏罚制度，歪门邪道反而增进；人们在处理人机关系时，会有亲疏远近之分，小人便可以趁机兴风作浪。若将金钱丢弃在大街上，盗贼也不敢去拾取；君王在朝堂上公开向众位大臣商讨政务，奸佞之人不敢进谗言了，天下就达到最公正的状态。

---

① 机：机理。
② 谋：图谋、筹划。

Chapter 57

Slanders

What is hidden and not shown is called the principle, and what is rare and precious and can win by surprise is called strategy. All people know the principles of great morality, but few people can act in accordance with benevolence and righteousness. Therefore, with the system of reward and punishment, evilness can succeed; as people always make a distinction between their close and distant relationships, the villain can take advantage of the opportunity to make mischief. If money is thrown out on the street, thieves will not dare to pick it up; if the king discusses government affairs openly with all the ministers in the court, treacherous people will not dare to slander, and the world will be in the most just state.

刻　画

画者不敢易^①于图象，苟易之，必有咎。刻者不敢侮于本偶，苟侮之，必贻祸。始制作于我，又要敬于我，又贻祸于我。是故张机者用于机，设险者死于险，建功者辱于功^②，立法者罹于法。动一窍则百窍相会，举一事则万事有害，所以机贵乎明，险贵乎平，功贵乎无状^③，法贵乎无象^④。能出刻画者，可以名之为大象^⑤。

·白话·

刻　画

作画的人不敢随意改变所绘神像的形象，若改变了，则必然会遭惩处；雕刻的匠人不敢轻慢对待自己雕刻的雕像，若轻慢了，必然留下祸患。它们一开始是由我制作出来的，我还要尊敬它们，它们还会给我带来祸害。因此，使用计谋的人被自己计谋所伤，设置陷阱的人被自己设置的陷阱所陷，立下功劳的人被自己的功劳所

---

①易：轻慢地对待。

②建功者辱于功，立法者罹于法：汉初韩信，三国时邓艾、钟会皆有功于朝，后竟不得善终；战国魏人李悝、秦之商鞅皆立主变法，虽于国于民有益，终因为权贵所不容，均遭罹难。

③无状：无功状，无成绩。

④无象：无物象。象，此指具体法律条文。

⑤大象：大道，常理。

害，立法的人最终被自己所立的法律制裁。变动一件事情的关窍则有成百件事情的关窍发生变化，发动一件事情则对千万的事情有损害。所以计谋重要的地方在于公开，陷阱重要的地方在于普通，功劳重要的地方在于没有凭证，法律重要的地方在于没有条律。能跳出雕刻和画像局限的，就可以称之为大道、常理。

Chapter **58**

Paintings and Carvings

He who paints gods does not dare to be careless about the image he paints; if he is careless, he is bound to be punished; the carver does not dare to trifle with the statue he carves; if he does, he is bound to leave a scourge. In the beginning things may be made by me, and I have to respect them, otherwise, they will bring me mischief. Thus, he who uses a scheme is injured by his own scheme, he who sets a trap is trapped by the trap he sets, he who makes a merit is harmed by his own merit, and he who legislates is eventually sanctioned by the law he makes. If one thing is changed, hundreds of other things will be changed in turn, and the practice of one thing may bring harm to millions of other things. Therefore, what is important about a scheme is that it should be open, what is important about a trap is that it should be ordinary, what is important about a merit is that there should be no proof, and what is important about laws is that there should be no written statutes. Those that can go beyond the limits of puinting and carving can be called the Tao.

酒　醴①

夫酒醴者，迫之饮愈不饮，恕之饮愈欲饮。是故抑人者人抑之，容人者人容之；贷②其死者乐其死，贷其输者乐其输。所以民盗③君之德，君盗民之力。能知反覆之道者，可以居兆民之职。

·白话·

酒　醴

对于喝酒的人来说，越是强迫他喝酒，他就越是不愿意喝，越是不让他喝酒，他就越是想要喝。因此压制别人的人也会受到别人的压制，宽容别人的人也得到别人的宽容；死罪得到宽恕的人死得心甘情愿，输钱得到豁免的人输得心甘情愿。所以百姓依靠君王的德行，君王依靠百姓的力量。能知道君王和百姓之间这种相互关系的人，就可以担任管理百姓的职位。

①醴：甜酒、美酒。
②贷：宽恕，宽免，饶恕。
③盗：借用。

Chapter 59

The Fine Wine

For a drinker of fine wine, the more he is forced to drink, the less he is willing to drink, and the more he is not allowed to drink, the more he wants to drink. Thus, he who bullies others is also bullied by others, and he who forgives others is forgiven by others; he who is forgiven for a deadly sin will die willingly, and he who is forgiven for losing money will lose it willingly without any grudges. So people count on the virtue of the emperor, and the emperor counts on the strength of the people. Only he who can realize the mutual relationship between the emperor and the people can take up the position of governing the people.

· 原文 ·

恩　赏

侯①者人所贵，金者人所重，众人封公②而得侯者不美，众人分玉而得金者不乐。是故赏不可妄行，恩不可妄施。其当也由为争夺之渐③，其不当也即为乱亡之基。故我自卑则赏不能大，我自俭则恩不得奇。历观乱亡之史皆骄侈，恩赏之所以为也。

· 白话 ·

恩　赏

王侯被人们尊重，金钱被人们看重，多数人被封赏了公爵，而只得到了侯爵的人就不满足；多数人分得了美玉，而只得到了黄金的人就不高兴。所以奖赏不能妄自执行，恩德不能妄自施加。赏罚使用恰当的，就成为争权夺利的发端；使用不恰当的，就成为引发国家动乱导致亡国的祸源。因此，自认谦卑，奖赏就不会过大；自身节俭，恩宠就不得特殊。历史上动乱亡国的，都是因为骄奢淫逸，君王溢加恩宠奖赏所造成的。

---

① 侯、公：古代五等爵制分为公、侯、伯、子、男五等。
② 侯、公：古代五等爵制分为公、侯、伯、子、男五等。
③ 渐：潜伏，通"潜"。

Chapter 60

Reward

Emperors and lords are respected by the people, and money is valued by the people. Those who receive the title of "Hou"[①] as a reward do not rejoice when everyone could get a title of "Gong", and those who receive gold as a reward do not feel joyful when everyone could get pearls and jade. Therefore, rewards and favors should not be bestowed indiscriminately. If rewards and punishments are used properly, they become the starting point of the struggle for power and profit; if they are used improperly, they become the source of national turmoil that leads to the downfall of the country. Therefore, the rewards would not be too great for those who consider themselves humble, and the favors would not be special for those who are frugal. All the downfalls of countries in history were caused by extravagance and indiscriminate favors and rewards from the emperor.

①Hou and Gong: The title-ranking system in Ancient China is divided titles into five classes—Gong (duke), Hou (marquis), Bo (earl), Zi (viscount) and Nan (baron).

化书之 **61**

· 原文 ·

养　民

民不怨火而怨使之禁火^①，民不怨盗而怨使之防盗。是故济民不如不济，爱民不如不爱。天有雨露，所以招其怨；神受祷祝，所以招其谤。夫禁民火不如禁心火，防人盗不如防我盗，其养民也如是。

· 白话 ·

养　民

百姓并不会怨恨火，而会怨恨那些禁止他们使用火的人；百姓并不会怨恨盗贼，而会怨恨那些使得他们不得不防范盗贼的人。因此救济百姓不如不救济，爱护百姓不如不爱护。天因为可以降下有雨水，所以招来了怨恨；神明因为接受百姓的祷祝，所以招来了诽谤。禁止百姓使用火不如消除百姓心中的不满，防范盗贼偷盗不如防范自身偷盗的念头。这也就是管理百姓的方法。

---

① 禁火：指禁止炊火。禁火为周朝的旧制度。旧俗寒食节禁火。

Chapter 61

Management

People do not resent fire, but hate those who prohibit them from using fire; people do not resent thieves, but resent those who make them guard against thieves. Therefore, it is better not to give relief to the people and not to take care of them. The rain often incurs resentment because it falls from the sky to the earth; the gods often incur slander because they accept the prayers of the people. It is better to eliminate the dissatisfaction of the people than to ban the people from using fire, and to prevent the thought of stealing than guard against thieves. This is the way to govern the people.

卷 四
Volume 4

仁　化

The Transformation of Benevolence

化书之 **62**

· 原文 ·

得 一①

　　旷然无为之谓道，道能自守之谓德，德生万物之谓仁，仁救安危之谓义，义有去就之谓礼，礼有变通之谓智，智有诚实之谓信，通而用之之谓圣。道，虚无也，无以自守，故授之以德。德，清静也，无以自用，故授之以仁。仁用而万物生，万物生必有安危，故授之以义。义济安拔危，必有藏否，故授之以礼。礼秉规持范，必有疑滞，故授之以智。智通则多变，故授之以信，信者，成万物之道也。

· 白话 ·

得 一

　　心性豁达，清静无为，就称为道；心地能长久保持住豁达无为状态，就称为德；由于豁达无为不干扰自然规律的运行，有利于万物生发，称为仁；由于有仁爱之心而救困拔厄，称为义；使义有表现形的，称为礼；能对礼根据情况变通施行，称为智；在这样的变通中保持诚实，称为信；将道德仁义礼智信贯通融合在一起，就称为圣。道即是虚无，而虚无是没有办法长久保持住的，因此虚无就将自己的特性赋

----

① "一"为数之始，又为物之极。得一，即得到纯正大道的意思。

予了德；德即是清净无为，而清静无为没有体现其作用，于是就需要仁；由于仁促进了万物生长发育，万物生长发育过程中必然有不利的事情发生，于是把义的功能加之于它；由于义是济安拔危，必然有褒贬品评，因此义就需要加上礼；礼是根据一定的规范决定济安拔危实施与否，必然有疑惑或停滞之处，因此礼又需要智的功能；智即是变通，由于变通太多使得事情无法确定下来，因此智需要加上信。信，即诚实，成为万物共同的大道。

Chapter 62

The Acquisition of Pure Taoism

Being generous, calm and non-active is called Tao, and being able to maintain the state of generosity, calmness and non-action is called Virtue. Thanks to the generosity and non-action, the natural law is not interrupted, which is beneficial to the growth of the nature, and it is called Benevolence. The action to save people from difficulties and troubles out of benevolence is called the Righteousness; and helping people but not indiscriminately is called Ritual; Being flexible when performing Rituals is called Wisdom; Being honest while being flexible is called the Faithfulness; Blending the Taoism, Virtue, Benevolence, Righteousness, Ritual, Wisdom and Faithfulness together is called Holiness. Taoism is nothingness, but there is no way to maintain nothingness for a long time. Therefore, nothingness needs Virtue.Virtue is purity and non-action, and the role of non-action is not easily detected, so Benevolence is added to it; since Benevolence promotes the growth and development of all things, and there are inevitably unfavorable things in the process, so Righteousness is added to it; since Righteousness is to ensure safety and prevent danger, there are inevitably praises and blames, so Ritual is added to it; Ritual is to decide

whether or not to help the people according to certain norms, and it must have doubts and hesitations, so Wisdom is added to it; Wisdom is to adapt, but too many adaptations make things too fickle, so Faithfulness is added to it. Faithfulness, that is, honesty, has become the common Tao of all things.

化书之**63**

· 原文 ·

五　行

　　道德者，天地也。五常①者，五行也。仁，发生之谓也，故均于木。义，救难之谓也，故均于金。礼，明白之谓也，故均于火。智，变通之谓也，故均于水。信，悫②然之谓也，故均于土。仁不足则义济之，金伐木也。义不足则礼济之，火伐金也。礼不足则智济之，水伐火也。智不足则信济之，土伐水也。始则五常相济之业，终则五常相伐之道，斯大化之往也。

· 白话 ·

五　行

　　道德即天地，五常即五行。五常中的仁，有利于万物生长发育，因此对应于五行中的木；五常中的义，救难拔厄，因此对应于五行中的金；五常中的礼，通彻光明，因此对应于五行中的火；五常中的智，变化通达，因此对应于五行中的水；五常中的信，意为诚实，因此对应于五行中的土。当仁不足的时候，义来补充，即为金克木；义不足的时候，礼来补充，即为火克金；礼不足的时候，智来补充，即为

①五常：仁、义、礼、智、信。
②悫（què）：诚实。

水克火；智不足的时候，信来补充，即为土克水。仁义礼智信顺序作用是五常相互补充，逆序作用则是五常相克。这亦是万物衍化的规律与趋势。

Chapter **63**

Wuxing

Morality is Heaven and Earth, and Five Virtues is Wuxing. Benevolence is beneficial to the growth of all things, which corresponds to Wood in Wuxing; The Righteousness in Five Virtues can save people from difficulties and dangers, which corresponds to Metal in Wuxing; The Ritual in Five Virtues means being bright and clear, which corresponds to Fire in Wuxing; The Wisdom in Five Virtues means being flexible in different situations, which corresponds to Water in Wuxing; Faithfulness in Five Virtues means being honest, which corresponds to Earth in Wuxing.

When Benevolence is insufficient, Righteousness will supplement it, that is, Metal will restrain Wood; When Righteousness is insufficient, Ritual will supplement it, that is, Fire will restrain Gold; When Ritual is insufficient, Wisdom will supplement it, that is, Water will restrain Fire; When Wisdom is insufficient, Faith will supplement it, that is, Earth will restrain Water. If Benevolence, Righteousness, Ritual, Wisdom and Faithfulness work in sequence, it means that they will complement each other. However, if they work in reverse order, it means that they will restrain each other. This is the way all things grow and develop.

畋 渔①

夫禽兽之于人也何异？有巢穴之居，有夫妇之配，有父子之性，有死生之情。乌反哺，仁也；隼②悯胎，义也；蜂有君③，礼也；羊跪乳，智也；雉④不再接，信也。孰究其道？万物之中五常百行无所不有也，而教之为网罟⑤，使之务畋渔。且夫焚其巢穴，非仁也；夺其亲爱，非义也；以斯为享，非礼也；教民残暴，非智也；使万物怀疑，非信也。夫膻⑥臭之欲不止，杀害之机不已。羽毛⑦虽无言，必状我为贪狼⑧之与封豕；鳞介⑨虽无知，必名我为长鲸⑩之与巨虺也。胡为自安，焉得不耻？吁！直疑自古无君子。

① 畋渔：打猎和捕鱼。
② 隼：鸟名。鸟类的一科，翅膀窄而尖，上嘴呈钩曲状，背青黑色，尾尖白色，腹部黄色。饲养驯熟后，可以帮助打猎。亦称"鹘"。
③ 蜂有君：每群蜂仅有一个雌蜂，居巢内产卵，他蜂附之组成群体，俗称蜂王。
④ 雉：鸟名。鹞鸡类，雄者羽色美丽，尾长，可作装饰品；雌者羽黄褐色，尾较短。汉人避吕后讳，称雉为"野鸡"。
⑤ 罟：网的通称。
⑥ 膻：此处代指野味、美味。
⑦ 羽毛：代指鸟类。
⑧ 贪狼：狼性贪婪。封豕：大猪。常用以喻贪暴者。
⑨ 鳞介：泛指有鳞和介甲的水生动物。
⑩ 长鲸：即鲸鱼，因其身巨长，故称。虺：毒蛇，大者长八九尺，扁头大眼，色如泥土。

·白话·

畋 渔

禽兽与人类有什么异同呢？禽兽有巢穴用来居住，有雌雄之间交配，有父子之间性情，有生离死别的情绪。鸟雏长大，衔食反哺其母，是仁；鹰隼捕猎时不捕捉怀胎的禽兽，是义；蜂群有自己的蜂王，是礼；母羊在哺乳羔羊时前腿跪下，是智；野鸡除配偶不交接第二个异性，是信。谁能探究这些禽兽的道呢？世界万物之中，仁义礼智信这五常在百行中无所不有，然而"君子"却教会百姓织网，使得百姓能捕鱼打猎。焚毁禽兽们居住的巢穴，是不仁；猎取禽兽们的幼子或配偶，是不义；以残害禽兽为自己享乐，是不礼；教唆人们变得残暴，是不智；使万物之间失去信任，相互怀疑，是不信。口腹之欲无休无止，猎取和残害禽兽的心思念念不已。飞禽虽然不会说话，但必然会将我们想象成贪得无厌的豺狼和残暴的山猪；鱼类和介甲动物虽然没有意识，必然也会将我们当成水里的大鲸和地上的巨蟒。对这样的情况我们竟然还安然自得，不感觉到羞耻？我真怀疑自古以来是不是没有出现过有学问有修养的人啊。

Chapter 64

Fishing and Hunting

What are the differences between animals and humans? Animals live in nests, and males mate with females. They enjoy love between father and son, and have emotions about life and death. When a bird grows up and feeds its mother, it is Benevolence; when a falcon hunts and does not catch a pregnant animal, and it is Righteousness; when the bees get themselves a queen, it is Ritual; when a ewe kneels on her front legs while nursing a lamb, it is Wisdom; when a pheasant does not mate with pheasants other than its mate, it is Faithfulness. Who can figure out the Tao of these beasts? The Five Virtues of Benevolence, Righteousness, Ritual, Wisdom and Faithfulness are found in all things in the world, but people are taught to weave nets so that they can fish and hunt. It is not benevolent to burn the nests where the animals live; it is unrighteous to hunt the young or mates of the animals; it is not courteous to mutilate the animals for one's own pleasure; it is unwise to instigate people to become brutal; it is treacherous to make all things lose trust in each other and to be suspicious of each other. The desire for food and drink is endless, and the thought of hunting and mutilating beasts is unceasing. The flying birds, though they cannot speak, will certainly compare us to the insatiable wolves and brutal pigs; the fish and crustaceans, though they are not conscious, will certainly compare us to the whales in the water and the pythons on the ground. How can we still feel comfortable with such a situation and not feel ashamed? I really wonder if there has not been a learned and cultivated people since ancient times.

化书之 **65**

·原文·

牺 牲

牺牲①之享②，羔雁③之荐④，古之礼也。且古之君子，非不知情之忧喜、声之哀乐能动天地、能感鬼神。刀杌⑤前列，则忧喜之情可知矣；鹰犬齐至，则哀乐之声可知矣。以是祭天地，以是祷神明，天地必不享，苟享之必有咎；神明必不歆⑥，苟歆之必有悔。所以知神龙⑦见，丧风云⑧之象也；凤凰⑨来，失尊戴之象也；麒麟⑩出，亡国土之象也。观我之义，禽必不义也；以彼为祥，禽必不祥也。

·白话·

牺 牲

供神享用的祭品，都是用羔羊和大雁，这是自古以来的礼制规矩。而且自古以

---

① 牺牲：牺，供祭祀用的纯色全体牲畜；牲，供食用和祭祀用的家畜。

② 享：供献，指把祭品、珍品献给祖先、神明或天子、侯王。

③ 羔雁：小羊和雁，古代卿大夫相见时所执的礼品。

④ 荐：献，进。

⑤ 杌：小凳子。

⑥ 歆：歆享。指鬼神享用祭品。

⑦ 神龙：古以龙为神物，称龙为神龙。

⑧ 风云：此处喻局势。

⑨ 凤凰：凰本作"皇"。传说中之鸟名。雄曰凤，雌曰凰。

⑩ 麒麟：传说中仁兽名。雄曰麒，雌曰麟，其状麋身、牛尾、狼蹄、一角。

来有学问有修养的人，并非不知道忧愁喜悦的情绪、哀伤欢乐的声音能够上达神明，感动天地。刀枪剑戟兵器阵列在前面，就可以知道是忧愁还是喜悦；鹰和犬都来到，就可以知道声音是哀伤还是欢乐。用带有这样情绪的祭品来祭天地，向神明祷祝，天地必然不会享用，若享用的话必然有灾难；神明也必然不会喜爱，若享用的话必然有悔恨。所以知道若是看见了神龙，就是神龙丧失了叱咤风云能力的征兆；若是看见凤凰飞来，就是凤凰丧失了百禽的尊敬和拥戴的征兆；若是麒麟出现，就是国家将要灭亡的征兆。对人来说是义的事情，对禽兽来说就是不义的事情；对人来说是吉祥的东西，对禽兽来说必然就是不吉详的东西。

Chapter 65

Sacrificial Offerings

Lambs and geese are used as sacrificial offerings for the gods. This has been a ritual since ancient times. Moreover, it is not that people who are learned and cultivated since ancient times do not know that sad and joyful emotions, sad and happy voices can reach the gods and move the heaven.With the array of swords, guns, swords, and halberds laid in front in a Sacrificial Ritual, you can tell whether people are sad or joyful; when the eagles and dogs appear in a Sacrificial Ritual, you can tell whether the sound is sad or joyful. If you offer sacrifices with such emotions to heaven and earth and pray to the gods, heaven and earth will certainly not enjoy them, and if they do, there will be disasters; and if the gods enjoy them, there will be remorse. Seeing the dragon is a symbol that the dragon will lose the ability to reign; seeing the phoenix fly is a symbol that the phoenix will lose the respect and support of all the birds; seeing the unicorn is a symbol that the country will be destroyed. What is righteous to men is unrighteous to beasts; what is auspicious to men is inevitably inauspicious to beasts.

化书之**66**

·原文·

太 和①

非兔狡，猎狡也；非民诈，吏诈也。慎勿怨盗贼，盗贼惟我召；慎勿怨叛乱，叛乱禀我教。不有和睦，焉得仇雠②；不有赏劝，焉得斗争。是以大人无亲无疏，无爱无恶，是谓太和。

·白话·

太 和

并不是兔子狡猾，而是猎人狡猾；并不是百姓奸诈，而是官吏奸诈。不要怨恨盗贼，盗贼都是自己招来的；不要怨恨叛乱，叛乱是秉承自己教化的结果。没有和睦，哪来的仇恨；没有赏罚，哪里来的争斗。于是道德高深之人没有远近和亲疏之分，没有爱恶之分，这就是太和。

---

①太和：天下太平、和睦。
②雠：同"仇"。

Chapter 66

Tai He[①]

It is not the hare that is cunning, but the hunter; it is not the people that are treacherous, but the officials. Do not resent the thief, for we invite the thief to come; do not resent the rebellion, for we teach people to rebel. Without harmony, there is no hatred; without reward and punishment, there is no strife. Therefore, to a highly moral person, there is no distinction between those who are close and those who are distant, and no distinction between love and hate. This is called Tai He.

①Tai He: Harmony and peace of the world.

化书之**67**

·原文·

墨 鱼

海鱼有吐墨水上庇其身而游者，人因墨而渔之。夫智者多屈，辩者多辱，明者多蔽，勇者多死。扃鐍①固，贼盗喜；忌讳严，敌国幸。禁可以越者，号也；兵可以夺者，符也。蜀败于山，晋败于马。夫大人之机，道德仁义而已矣。

·白话·

墨 鱼

海里有一种鱼，在游动的时候吐出墨水来隐蔽自己，人们因为想要它的墨水而专门捕捞它。聪明才智出众的人大多屈居人下，能言善辩的人大多遭受折辱，贤明大度的人大多受到欺瞒，英勇善战的人大多不得善终。门窗箱柜上的锁具越牢固，盗贼就越欢喜；严禁的东西越多，敌对国家就越感到庆幸。可以违反禁令的，是军队的号角；可以夺取军队指挥权的，是兵符。蜀国由于山地围绕而灭亡，晋国由于依仗分立诸王，后起战乱而灭亡。道德高深之人处事成功的关键，不过就是运用道德仁义而已。

---

①鐍：指门栓

Chapter 67

Cuttlefish

There is a type of fish in the sea that release ink to conceal themselves when they swim, and there are people who specialize in catching them because they want the ink. Most of those who are clever and wise will be subordinate to others; most of those who are eloquent will be humiliated; most of those who are wise and generous will be deceived; and most of those who are brave will not end well. The stronger the doors, windows and chests are locked, the more the thieves will be attracted; the more there are things in a country that are strictly forbidden, the more their hostile nations will feel glad. What can violate the prohibition is the trumpet of the army; what can seize the command of the army is the commander's seal. The State of Shu[①] fell because of the mountains surrounding it, and the State of Jin[②] fell because its people were not united. The key to the success of a highly morally person in dealing with affairs is nothing more than the use of Virtue, Benevolence and Righteousness.

---

①Shu and Jin are all dynasties in Chinese history. Here it says the State of Shu fell because of the mountains surrounding it. Zhua Geliang had commanded his army and tried six times to fight out the encirclement of mountains but all failed, which led to the fall of the State of Shu.

②The State of Jin fell: It refers to the emperor of the state of Jin, Zhi Yao, who was skilled in bow and horse shooting. He held himself strong and bullied Han, Wei and Zhao, but was defeated by the united three states, and the state of Jin was finally destroyed.

化书之**68**

·原文·

神 弓

誉人者人誉之，谤人者人谤之，是以君子能罪己，斯罪人也；不报怨，斯报怨也。所谓神弓鬼矢，不张而发，不注①而中。天得之以假②人，人得之以假天下。

·白话·

神 弓

总是称赞他人的人，也会受到他人的称赞；总是诋毁他人的人，也会受到他人的诋毁；因此有学问有道德之人把过失归到自己身上，就等于把过失归到他人身上；不抱怨他人，就等于抱怨他人。这就是所说的神弓鬼矢，不需要张弓就可以发射出箭矢，不需要瞄准就可以射中目标。上天得到它就可以用它来控制人，人得到它就可以用它来控制天下。

---

①注：投，掷，这里指射箭。
②假：给予，施予。

Divine Bow

He who always praises others will also be praised by others; he who always denigrates others will also be denigrated by others. Therefore, the learned and moral person who attributes faults to himself is actually attributing faults to others; he who does not complain about others is actually complaining about others. This is the so called "divine bow and arrow", which can fire an arrow without pulling the string and hit the target without aiming. When the heaven gets it, it can be used to control man, and when man gets it, he can use it to control the world.

化书之 **69**

救 物

救物而称义者，人不义之；行惠而求报者，人不报之。民之情也，让之则多，争之则少，就之则去，避之则来；与之则轻，惜之则夺。是故大义无状，大恩无象。大义成，不知者荷之；大恩就，不识者报之。

救 物

援助别人物品而自称义举的人，众人并不因其行为而称之为义举；对别人施了恩惠后要求回报的人，众人并不因此其施惠回报他。百姓的性情是：谦让时东西就会很多，争夺时东西就会很少，想要得到东西的时候就会失去，躲避的时候东西就会自己找上来；赠与的东西被轻视，珍惜的东西被争夺。因此大义没有具体的行为状态，大恩没有具体的形象。成就了大义还不知道的，会受到感谢；成就了大恩还不知道的，会受到报答。

Chapter 69

The Help

He who saves the property of others and calls himself righteous will not be considered righteous by others; and he who does good to others and expects a reward will not be rewarded by others. This is the nature of the people. When they are humble, they have much, and when they fight, they have little; when they want something, they lose it, and when they elude it, it comes to them; what is given is despised, and what is cherished is fought for. Thus, great righteousness has no specific state of action, and great kindness has no specific image. Those who achieve great righteousness without knouing it will be thanked, and those who perform acts of great kindness without realizing it will be rewarded.

·原文·

书 道

心不疑乎手，手不疑乎笔，忘手笔，然后知书之道。和畅，非巧也；淳古，非朴也；柔弱，非美也；强梁，非勇也。神之所浴，气之所沐。是故点策蓄血气，顾盼含情性。无笔黑之迹，无机智之状；无刚柔之容，无驰骋之象。若皇帝之道熙熙然，君子之风穆穆然。是故观之者，其心乐，其神和，其气融，其政太平，其道无朕。夫何故？见山思静，见水思动，见云思变，见石思贞，人之常也。

·白话·

书 道

心不怀疑手，手也不怀疑心，心与手合一，手与笔合一，忘掉手和笔，然后才可以明白书法的大道。融和顺畅，并非就是灵敏机巧；醇厚质朴有古风，并非就是朴实；柔弱，并非就是美丽；粗暴凶狠，并非就是勇敢。由于意识笼罩，元气熏陶，所以出谋划策中含有血气在内，接人待物中含有性情在内。没有笔墨留下的痕迹，就没有机心智谋的形状；没有刚强柔弱的容貌，就没有驰骋万里的形状。要像皇帝之道那样温和欢悦，像有道德有学问之人的风格那样端庄宁静。因此能看到这些事情本质的人，心地愉悦欢欣，精神平和无波，气色和谐，执政盛世太平，处事无兆无象。什么原因呢？看见山的时候心里就会安静，看见水的时候心里就会发生波动，看见云的时候心里就会产生变化，看见石头的时候心里就会变得坚定，这就是人之常情。

Chapter 70

Calligraphy

The heart does not suspect the hand, nor does the hand suspect the heart. The heart is united with the hand, the hand is united with the brush. Forgetting about the hand and the brush, and then you can get the way of calligraphy. To be harmonious and smooth is not to be agile and sensitive; to be mellow and rustic is not to be plain; to be soft is not to be beautiful; to be rough and fierce is not to be brave.

Under the influence of the spirit and Yuanqi, there is blood in the strategy, and there is temperament in the treatment of people. There are no traces left by ink and brush, no shape of wit and wisdom, no appearance of strength and weakness, no form of galloping for miles. It is to be as gentle and joyful as the way of the emperor, and as dignified and tranquil as the style of a moral and learned man. Therefore, those who can see the essence of these things have a pleasant and joyful heart, a calm and unruffled spirit, and a harmony within, and they rule a prosperous and peaceful world, and deal with things without signs or images. Why is this so? It is common that when you see mountains, your heart becomes quiet; when you see running water, your heart fluctuates; when you see clouds, your heart changes, and when you see stones, your heart becomes firm.

化书之**71**

凤 鸥

凤不知美，鸥①不知恶，陶唐氏②不知圣，有苗氏③不知暴。使陶氏恃其圣，非圣也；有苗氏知其暴，不暴也。众人皆能写人之形，而不能写己之形；皆能求人之恶，而不能求己之恶；皆能知人之祸，而不能知己之祸。是以大人听我声，察我色，候我形，伺我气，然后知人之情伪④。

凤 鸥

凤凰不知道自己美丽，鸥鹰不知道自己凶恶，上古时期陶唐氏不知道自己的圣明，有苗氏不知道自己残暴。若陶唐氏自恃他的圣明，就不是圣人了；若有苗氏知道自己残暴，就不会残暴了。众人都能够描述他人的形象，而不能描述自己的形象；都能挑剔他人的毛病，而不能挑剔自己的毛病；都能知道他人的灾祸，而不能知道自己的灾祸。因此道德高深之人倾听自己的声音，观察自己的气色，审察自己的形

---

① 鸥：鸥鹰。
② 陶唐氏：帝尧，初居于陶，后封于唐，为唐侯，故称。
③ 有苗氏：即三苗。我国古代部族名。
④ 情伪：真假。

体，调理自己的元气，然后就能借此推知人情中的真假。

Chapter 71

The Phoenix and the Sparrow Hawk

The phoenix does not know its beauty, the sparrow hawk does not know its viciousness. In ancient times, the Tao Tang clan did not know they were uise, the Miao clan did not know they were brutal. If the Tao Tang clan think too much of themselves because their clan was wise, they would not be sages any longer; if the Miao knew that they were brutal, they would not be brutal. All people are able to describe the image of others, but not of their own; all people are able to pick on the faults of others, but not of their own; all people are able to recognize the calamities of others, but not of their own. Therefore the morally high person listens to his own voice, observes his own complexion, watches his own form, and regulates his own Yuanqi, and then he can use it to identify the true and false in human affairs.

化书之 **72**

· 原文 ·

知 人

观其文章，则知其人之贵贱焉；观其书篆，则知其人之情性焉；闻其琴瑟，则知其人之道德焉；闻其教令，则知其人之吉凶焉。小人由是知唐尧之容淳淳①然，虞舜之容熙熙然，伯禹之容荡荡②然，殷汤之容堂堂③然，文王之容巍巍④然，武王之容谔谔⑤然，仲尼之容皇皇⑥然。则天下之人，可以自知其愚与贤。

· 白话 ·

知 人

阅读了一个人写的文章，就可以知道其人格是尊贵还是卑贱；看了一个人的书法篆刻，就可以知道他的性情如何；听了一个人用琴瑟弹奏的音乐，就可以知道他的道德修养如何；听闻到一个人颁布的法令，就可以知道他的吉凶如何。人们于是知道，唐尧时代的社会民风淳朴自然，虞舜时代的社会民风快乐无忧，伯禹时代的

① 淳淳：流畅、畅通无阻
② 荡荡：广远的样子。
③ 堂堂：事物庄严、壮大
④ 巍巍：高大的样子。
⑤ 谔谔：直言、正直。
⑥ 皇皇：求而不得的样子。

社会民风坦坦荡荡，殷汤时代的社会民风庄严大方，文王时代社会民风高大巍然，武王时代民风刚直不阿，仲尼时代社会民风惶惶不安。因此天下之人就可以知道自己是贤达还是愚昧了。

Chapter **72**

Distinguishing People

When I read a person's writings, I can tell whether his character is noble or poor; when I read a person's calligraphy or seal engravings, I can tell what his disposition is; when I listen to the music of a person playing on his zither, I can tell what his moral cultivation is; when I hear the decrees a ruler issued, I can tell what his fortune is. Then I get to know that the society in the time of Yao was simple and natural, the society in the time of Shun was happy and carefree, the society in the time of Yu was frank and open, the society in the time of emperor Tang in Yin Dynasty was solemn and generous, the society in the time of emperor Wen in Zhou Dynasty was high and lofty, the society in the time of emperor Wu was straight and upright, and the society in the time of emperor Wu in Zhou Dynasty was full of fear. Thus the people of the world could know whether the rulers were virtuous or foolish.

化书之 **73**

·原文·

蝼 蚁

蝼蚁之有君也，一拳之宫，与众处之；一块之台，与众临之；一粒之食，与众蓄之，一虫之肉，与众咂①之；一罪之疑，与众戮之。故得心相通而后神相通。神相通而后气相通，气相通而后形相通。故我病则众病，我痛则众痛，怨何由起，叛何由始？斯太古②之化也。

·白话·

蝼 蚁

小如蝼蚁也有自己的君王。即使是一拳大小的王宫，也会与众蝼蚁相处在一起；即使是一块小小的台子，也会与众蝼蚁一起上去；即使是米粒大小的食物，也会与众蝼蚁一起蓄积；即使是一条小虫子的肉，也会与众蝼蚁一起共享；即使是发现一条罪状，也会与众蝼蚁一起共同讨伐。因此得到心灵相通而后精神相通，精神相通而后气性相通，气性相通而后形体相通。若是一人病则众人皆病，一人痛则众人皆痛，这样百姓怎么会产生怨恨，怎么会发生叛乱呢？这都是太古时代的民风教化。

---

① 咂：吸吮。
② 太古：远古，上古。

Chapter 73

The Ants

Even small ants have their own emperor. Though the emperor's palace is only fist-sized, all the ants can get along well in it; though a platform is only a small stone, all the ants will go up on it; though the food is as little as a grain, it will be stored by all the ants; though the meat is as small as a worm, it will still be shared by all the ants together; even if a crime is found, it will be judged together by all the ants. Therefore, when the mind is connected, the spirit will be connected, when the spirit is connected, Qi will be connected, and when Qi is connected, the form will be connected. If one person is sick, all people will be sick, and if one person is in pain, all people will be in pain, so how can resentment arise and how can rebellion occur? This is the civil culture of the ancient times.

化书之 **74**

· 原文 ·

歌 舞

能歌者不能者听之，能舞者不能者观之，巧者不巧者辨之，贤者不贤者任之。夫养木者必将伐之，待士者必将死之。网之以冠冕，钓之以爵禄。若马驾车辂，贵不我得；彘食糟糠，肥不我有。是以大人道不虚贵，德不虚守；贫有所倚，进有所恃，退者非乐寒贱而甘委弃。

· 白话 ·

歌 舞

歌手为不会唱的人唱歌，舞姬为不会舞的人跳舞，善言辞的被不善言辞的评判，贤达的被不贤达的驱使。种树的必将砍树，优待武士的必将用武士为之赴死。以高官爵位为网来捕，以厚禄待遇为饵来钓。就像豪华车驾虽然尊贵，却不是驾车的马所能得到的；就像食糟糠的猪虽然肥，猪肉却不属于猪。因此道德高深之人修道不追求无用的地位尊贵，坚持自己的德行必要落到实地，贫困时修行可以作为依靠，发展上升时修行可以作为后盾，在后退时，也不是想以贫寒卑贱为乐，甘心遭受弃置。

Chapter 74

Singing and Dancing

Singers sing for those who cannot sing, dancers dance for those who cannot dance, eloquent people are judged by people who are not eloquent, and the virtuous are driven by those who are not virtuous. Those who plant trees will cut the trees down, and those who treat warriors favorably will make those warriors die for them. A high official title is used as a net, and a generous salary is used as bait. Just as a luxurious carriage, though noble, does not belong to the horse driving it; just as a pig that eats chaff, though fat, does not possess its own meat. Therefore, a person with high morality does not pursue useless status and honor, but insists that his virtue must be put into practice, so that his practice can be relied on when he is poor, and can be used as a backup when he rises. When he retreats, he does not take pleasure in being poor or willingly be abandoned.

化书之 **75**

踯 躅①

踯躅之酒，乌喙之脯，莨菪②之膏，冶葛③之乳。初啖④之若芥，再啖之若黍，复啖之若丸⑤，又啖之若脯。小人由是知强弩⑥可以渐引，巨鼎可以渐举，水火可以渐习，虎兕⑦可以渐侣。逆者我所化，辱者我所与，不应者我所命，不臣者我所取。所以信柔马不可驭，渐贼不可御。得之以为万化之母。

踯 躅

用杜鹃花酿制的酒，乌鸦嘴做的肉脯，莨菪草榨出的油脂，冶葛草挤出的汁液。初次吃它的时候味道如芥草一样苦涩，再吃的时候味道就变得像黄米，第三次吃的时候味道就变得像蛋卵，第四次吃的时候味道就变得像肉脯。人们由此知道，强力

---

① 踯躅：花名，即杜鹃花。

② 莨菪：草名。

③ 冶葛：草名。

④ 啖：食。

⑤ 丸：卵。

⑥ 弩：用机械发射的弓，也叫窝弓，力强可趴及远。其种类很多，大者或用脚踏，或用腰开，有数矢并发者称连弩。

⑦ 兕：兽名。似牛。古书常犀兕并举，或说兕即雌犀。

的弓弩可以一点一点的拉开，巨大沉重的铜鼎可以一点一点的举起来，水深火热可以一点一点的习惯，虎豹猛兽可以一点一点的驯服。叛逆我的我可以逐渐将他转化，侮辱我的正是我所要亲附的，不服从的我可以使他逐渐听从命令，不称臣不屈服的我可以逐渐使他屈服。所以我相信柔弱的马不可驾驭，逐渐成形的贼盗不可抵御。懂得这个道理，可以把握万物化育的本真。

Chapter 75

Azaleas

There are some food such as the wine made from azalea, the dried meat made from crow's beak, the cream from the herb of henbane seed, and the herbal juice of kudzu. When you first have them, they taste as bitter as grass; when you have them again, they taste like rice; when you have them for the third time, they taste like eggs, and when you have them for the fourth time, they taste like dried meat. From this, people get to know that the powerful bow can be drawn little by little; the huge and heavy bronze tripod can be lifted up little by little; the tiger and leopard can be tamed day by day, and people can become accustomed to harsh conditions day by day. For those who are rebellious, I can gradually convert them; for those who used to insult me, I can gradually follow them; for those who are disobedient, I can gradually make them obey orders; for those who are unyielding, I can gradually make them submit.That is why I believe that a weak horse cannot be harnessed, a thief that is made gradually cannot be guarded against. The one who understands this can grasp the true nature of the transformation and development of all things.

化书之**76**

·原文·

止 斗

止人之斗者使其斗，抑人之忿者使其忿；善救斗者预其斗，善解忿者济其忿。是故心不可伏，而伏之愈乱；民不可理，而理之愈怨。水易动而自清，民易变而自平。其道也在不逆万物之情。

·白话·

止 斗

制止别人争斗的人先让别人争斗，平抑别人忿怒的人先让别人忿怒；善于调解争斗的人参与争斗，善于平抑别人忿怒的人火上浇油。因此，人心是不可以被强制屈服的，愈是强制愈是叛逆；百姓是不可以治理的，愈是想治理愈是有怨恨。水本性易于流动因而可以自净自清，百姓心性易于变化因而可以自己平伏。其中的道理就在于不去违背万物自然规律。

Stopping Strife

He who wants to restrain others from strife should first make them fight, and he who wants to pacify people's anger should first make them angry; he who is good at mediating fights participates in it, and he who is good at pacifying their anger intensifies it. Therefore, people cannot be forced to submit, because the more they are forced, the more they rebel; the people cannot be controled, because the more you try to control them, the more they resent you. Water is by nature easy to flow and therefore can purify itself, and the people's hearts are easy to change and therefore can calm themselves. The truth lies in not doing things against the natural laws of all things.

化书之 **77**

· 原文 ·

象 符

术有降万物之蕴毒者，则交臂钩指，象之为符。是故若夭矫[①]之势者鳞[②]之符，若飞腾之势者羽[③]之符，若偃蹇[④]之势者毛之符，若拳跼[⑤]之势者介之符，所以知拱折者人之符。夫拱手者，人必拱之；折腰者，人必折之，礼之本也。而疏之为万象，别之为万态。教之蹈舞，非蹈舞[⑥]也；使之祷祝，非祷祝也，我既寡实，彼亦多虚。而责人之无情，固无情也；而罪礼之无验，固无验也。

· 白话 ·

象 符

道术之中，有一种可以解除万物中蕴含的毒性的方法，由道人手臂相交、手指勾起形成一种符象。因此，如果姿态矫健、屈伸自如的为鳞鱼符，如果姿态好像飞

① 夭矫：是指伸展自如的样子。
② 鳞：是指对所有的有鳞的动物的一种统称。
③ 羽：是对所有鸟类的统称。
④ 偃蹇：指屈曲。
⑤ 拳跼：指局促得不到伸展。
⑥ 蹈舞：臣下朝贺时对皇帝表示敬意的一种礼节。

腾要起飞的样子，是鸟类符；如果姿态好像是要扑倒的样子的，是兽类符，如果姿态好像很局促，不能伸展的，是介甲符，因此，知道拱手和折腰的，是人类的符。若你别人拱手致意，别人也会向你拱手致意；若你向别人弯腰鞠躬，别人也会向你弯腰鞠躬，这是礼制的本来意义。这种意义分散开，就会有千万种符号，区别开来，就会有千万种形态。硬逼别人去行蹈舞礼的，就体现不了蹈舞礼的真谛了；迫使别人去行祷告的仪式的，也必然达不到祷告的效果。自己若不是实心实意，他人也就必然虚情假意。而责备他人无情的，应该自己反省，自己本来也就无情；而怪罪他人礼节不周的应该反省，自己本来也就礼节不周。

Chapter 77

The Image of Fu①

In Taoism, there is a method to remove the poison contained in all things — the Taoist's arms are interlocked and his fingers hooked together to form a Fu. Therefore, if the posture looks robust, free and flexible, it is the Fu of scaly fish; if the posture seems like being ready to take off, it is the Fu of birds; if the posture seems to pounce, it is the Fu of beasts; if the posture seems to be confined and cannot be stretched, it is the Fu of shelled animals. If you arch your hands in greeting others, others will also arch their hands in greeting to you; if you bend and bow to others, others will also bend and bow to you, which is the original meaning of the ritual system. When this meaning is dispersed, it will become millions of

---

①Fu: In Taoism, Fu can be some pictures drawn by Taoists, or some postures formed by the body of the Taoist. The symbols of Fu are the medium of communication between man and god, and between man and the dominant power of the religious world; they are the embodiment of the super-inspired power of religion; they are the spiritual power of man's desire to overcome evil and disaster in the real world through other powers. In short, different images of Fu simbolize different things in Taoism.

symbols, and when it is made to be distinguished, it will take millions of forms. Those who force others to perform the ritual of dancing will not reflect the true meaning of the ritual; those who force others to perform the ritual of prayer will certainly not achieve the effect of prayer. If you are not sincere, others will be insincere. He who blames others for being heartless should reflect on himself, for he himself is certainly heartless; and he who blames others for being ill-mannered should reflect on himself, for he himself is ill-mannered.

善 恶

为恶者畏人识，必有识者；为善者欲人知，必有不知者。是故人不识者，谓之大恶；人不知者，谓之至善。好行惠者恩不广，务奇特者功不大，善博奕者智不远，文绮丽者名不久。是以君子惟道是贵，惟德自守，所以能万世不朽。

· 白话 ·

善 恶

做坏事的人怕别人认出来，但肯定会有人认出来；做善事的人想让别人知道，但肯定会有不知道的。因此，做坏事不被别人认出来的，就称之为大恶；做善事不为人所知的，就称之为至善。喜欢实施恩惠的，其恩惠不广博；追求出奇效果的，功劳也不会大；善于下棋的不会有远大智慧，用华丽辞藻做文章的，即使出名也是昙花一现。因此有道德修养的人以道为至上，坚守自己的德行，所以能够万世不朽。

Chapter 78

The Good Deeds and the Evil Deeds

Those who do evil things are afraid of being found out by others, but what they have done will certainly be found out some day; those who do good things want others to notice them, but there will certainly be those who will not notice. Therefore, the evil acts that people did without being found out by others are called the heinous acts; the nice deeds that people did without being noticed by others are called great deeds. He who likes to perform acts of kindness is not of great benevdence; he who pursues surprising effects will not have great merits; he who is good at chess will not have great wisdom; and he who uses magnificent rhetoric for his articles will only be famous transiently. Therefore, those who have moral cultivation take Tao as their supreme guideline and hold fast to their virtue, so they can be immortal for generations.

食　化

The Transformation of Food

化书之 79

七　夺

一日不食则惫，二日不食则病，三日不食则死。民事之急，无甚于食，而王者夺其一，卿士夺其一，兵吏夺其一，战伐夺其一，工艺夺其一，商贾夺其一，道释之族夺其一，稔亦夺其一，俭亦夺其一。所以蚕告终而缲葛苎之衣，稼云毕而饭橡栎之实。王者之刑理不平，斯不平之甚也；大人之道救不义，斯不义之甚也。而行切切之仁，用戚戚之礼，其何以谢之哉！

七　夺

一日不食就会疲惫不堪，二日不食就会发生疾病，三日不食就会导致死亡。百姓的事情之中，最急迫的莫过于饮食，然而国家君王掠夺一次，王公大臣掠夺一次，兵卒酷吏掠夺一次，战乱动荡掠夺一次，工矿艺技掠夺一次，富商大贾掠夺一次，儒道佛之族掠夺一次，丰年之年掠夺一次，歉收之年掠夺一次。所以织布的蚕丝用尽，百姓不得不用葛苎为衣，收获的粮食被掠夺一空，百姓不得不以橡栎果实充饥。君王的刑罚是为了治理不公平，但这才是极端的不公平；达官贵人们的道是为了补救不义，可这才是最大的不义。然而上者只忙于仁爱，紧张地施行礼仪，怎么能够洗刷掉罪过呢？

Chapter 79

Seven Times of Plundering

People will be exhausted if they do not eat for a day; they will get ill if they do not eat for two days; they may die if they do not eat for three days. Therefore, to a common people, food is their priority. However, the emperor of the country plunders them once; the princes and ministers plunder them once; the soldiers and cruel officials plunder them once; the war and turmoil plunder them once; the industry and mines plunder them once; the rich merchants plunder them once; the monks plunder them once; during year of good harvest, they get plundered once; during the year of bad harvest, they get plundered once. When the silk runs out, people will have to use ramie for clothes. When the harvested grain is plundered, people will have to feed on acorns. The rules and punishment of the emperors are made to manage the unfair, but this is even more unfair than those of others. The Tao of officials and aristocrats is to remedy injustice, but this injustice is even more extreme. So how can the sin be washed away with hurried benevolence and courtesy?

化书之 **80**

·原文·

巫　像

　　为巫者鬼必附之，设像者神必主之，盖乐所响也。戎羯之礼，事母而不事父；禽兽之情，随母而不随父；凡人之痛，呼母而不呼父，盖乳哺之教也。虎狼不过于嗜肉，蛟龙不过于嗜血，而人无所不嗜。所以不足则斗，不与则叛，鼓天下之怨，激烈士之忿。食之道非细①也。

·白话·

巫　像

　　有巫术的人鬼必然会附到他的身上，设立神像的人神必然会为他做主，这道理就像拨动乐器发出响声一样。戎羯等西北少数民族的礼制，只孝敬母亲而不孝敬父亲；禽兽之间，只随母而不随父；平常人遇到痛苦时，呼唤母亲而不呼唤父亲，这都是母亲哺乳教养的原因。虎狼只不过是嗜肉，蛟龙只不过是嗜血，而人却无所不嗜。所以，食物不足就引发争斗；得不到食物就叛乱，鼓动百姓的怨愤，激发壮士的愤怒。由此可知食物的作用一定要认真对待。

---

① 细：苛细、苛求。

Sorcery and Statue

A man with sorcery is bound to get possessed by ghosts, and a man who sets up an statue of a god is bound to have the gods help him, just as playing a musical instrument will make a loud sound. In the rituals of the minority group in Northwestern area such as Rong and Jie, they only honor their mothers but not their fathers. Among beasts, they only follow their mothers but not their fathers. For ordinary people, when they are in pain, they call on their mothers but not their fathers, and this is all because of their mothers' nursing and upbringing. Tigers and wolves just love to eat meat, dragons just love to drink blood, but people love to eat everything. Therefore, if there is not enough food, there will be fighting; if there is no food, there will be rebellion, and the people's grievances and the anger of the brave men will be aroused. This shows that the problem of food must be treated with care and cannot be ignored.

化书之 81

·原文·

养 马

养马者主，而牧之者亲；养子者母，而乳之者亲。君臣非所比，而比之者禄也；子母非所爱，而爱之者哺也。驽马本无知，婴儿本无机，而知由此始，机由此起。所以有爱恶，所以有彼此，所以稔①斗争而蓄奸诡。

·白话·

养 马

养马的人是马的主人，而牧马的人与马更亲近；扶养孩子的人是孩子的母亲，而奶妈与孩子更亲近。大臣听从君主命令并非是由于别的什么原因，而是由于君主给与大臣的俸禄；孩子之所以爱母亲，并非是由于别的什么原因，而是由于母亲的哺乳。柔弱的马本来没有智慧，婴儿本来没有机谋变化之心，而马的智慧由此开始产生，婴儿的机心由此发起。所以有了爱与恶的分别，所以有了彼此的分别，所以人与人之间的不断争斗，阴谋诡计不断积累。

---

① 稔：使事物不停酝酿成熟。

Horse Breeding

He who owns a horse is the master of the horse, but he who feeds and shepherds the horse is closer to the horse; the one who raises a child is the mother of the child, but the one who feeds and nurses the child is closer to the child. The minister obeys the ruler not for any other reason, but because of the salary the ruler gives to him; the child loves the mother not for any other reason, but because of the mother's nursing. Originally the weak horse has no intelligence, and the infant has no knowledge, but as time goes on, the horse develops intelligence, and the infant begins to acquire knowledge. There then emerges the difference between love and evil, between you and me, which leads to the constant accumulation of intrigue and trickery among people.

化书之 82

·原文·

丝 纶

王取其丝，吏取其纶[1]；王取其纶，吏取其綷[2]。取之不已，至于欺罔；欺罔不已，至于鞭挞；鞭挞不已，至于盗窃；盗窃不已，至于杀害；杀害不已，至于刑戮。欺罔非民爱，而哀[3]敛者教之；杀害非民愿，而鞭挞者训之。且夫火将逼而投于水，知必不免，且贵其缓；虎将噬而投于谷，知必不可，或觊其生。以斯为类，悲哉！

·白话·

丝 纶

君王夺取百姓的丝线，官吏就夺取百姓的纶带；君王夺取百姓的纶带，官吏就夺取百姓的绳索。不停的夺取下去，导致欺骗蒙蔽；不停的欺骗蒙蔽下去，导致鞭挞惩罚；不停的鞭挞惩罚下去，导致盗窃；不停的盗窃下去，导致杀害；不停的杀害下去，导致刑罚。欺罔并非是百姓故意而为的，而是聚敛民财的人迫使的；杀害并非是百姓愿意做的，而是鞭挞的人训练出来的。在大火焚烧的威胁下被迫跳到水

---

① 纶：质量相对比较差的一种丝。
② 綷：指绳索
③ 哀：聚集。

里，虽然知道不免一死，但却是可以缓上一些时间；面对吃人的老虎被迫跳下悬崖深谷，虽然知道跳下去可能会被摔死，但还是有一丝或许能够活命的希望。这与前面百姓的情况类似，多么可悲啊。

Chapter 82

The Silk

When the emperors rob the people of their silk, the officials rob the people of their Lun[①]; when the emperor rob the people of their Lun, the officials rob the people of their rope. Continuous robbing will lead to deceiving; continuous deceiving will lead to whipping and punishment; continuous whipping and punishment will lead to theft; continuous theft will lead to killing; continuous killing will lead to severe penalties. People do not intend to deceive deliberately, but are forced by those who amass the people's wealth; people do not intend to kill others willingly, but are taught by those who whip them. People who are forced to jump into the water under the threat of burning fire, although they know that they will not be spared from death, it is a way to slow down the dying time. People are forced to jump off a deep valley in the face of tiger, although they know that they might be killed by the fall, there is still a glimmer of hope that they might be able to live. This is similar to the previous situation. How sad it is.

①Lun: This is a type of silk in Ancient China, the quality of which is inferior to first-class silk.

化书之 **83**

奢 僭

夫君子不肯告人以饥，耻之甚也。又不肯矜人以饱，愧之甚也。既起人之耻愧，必激人之怨咎，食之害也如是。而金籩①玉豆，食之饰也；鼓钟戛②石，食之游也；张组设绣，食之惑也；穷禽竭兽，食之暴也；滋味厚薄，食之忿也；贵贱精粗，食之争也。欲之愈不止，求之愈不已，贫食愈不足，富食愈不美。所以奢僭由兹而起，战伐由兹而始。能均其食者，天下可以治。

奢 僭

有学问有修养的人不肯因自己饥饿向别人求告，是因自己饥饿而别人不饥饿感到耻辱；又不肯因自己饱食向别人显耀，是因自己已经饱食别人不饱食感到惭愧。既然引起了人的耻辱羞愧之心，必然会激起人的抱怨，这就是饮食带来的坏处。金丝编织的盛器和玉石制作的豆子，作为饮食的装饰；敲击钟鼓和响石，作为饮食期间的游戏；铺设华丽桌台，用来增加饮食的诱惑；过度狩猎各种禽兽，是因食物而

---

① 籩（biān）：即笾。古代祭祀和宴会时盛果品等的竹器。
② 戛（jiá）：敲击石头。

施行的残暴；计较食物味道的好坏，会产生忿恨；比较食物的贵贱精粗，会引起竞争。想要精美的饮食这种欲望越强烈，就越想方设法去获得，穷人的饮食就越不足，富人对饮食就越不满足。所以奢侈由此而产生，战争由此而开始。能够平均分配食物的人，才能治理好天下。

Chapter 83

Luxury

The learned and cultivated man refuses to ask others for food when he is hungry, because he is ashamed that he is hungry while others are not; and he will not show off to others when he is full, because he is guilty that he is full while others are not. Since it arouses shame in people, it will certainly provoke people to complain, and this is the negative effect of food. Rich people use golden silk vessels to hold food and beans made of jade to decorate food; beat bells and drums and rattle stones as a game during eating; lay magnificent tables and platforms to increase the temptation of eating; hunt excessively and commit atrocities for food. The difference in the taste of food will cause hatred among people; the difference in the quality of food will cause competition among people. The stronger the desire for fine food, the more one tries to get it, the more inadequate the food of the poor is, and the more dissatisfied the rich are with it. This is how luxury arises and war begins. He who can distribute food equally can rule the world well.

化书之 84

· 原文 ·

燔 骨①

　　嚼燔骨者，焦脣烂舌不以为痛；饮醇酎②者，哕③肠呕胃不以为苦。馋嗜者由忘于痛苦，饥穷者必轻于性命。痛苦可忘，无所不欺；性命可轻，无所不为。是以主者以我欲求人之欲，以我饥求人之饥。我怒民必怒，我怨民必怨。能知其道者，天下胡为乎叛？

· 白话 ·

燔 骨

　　啃烤肉骨头的人，烫的唇舌起泡也不觉得疼痛；饮美酒的人，翻肠倒胃的呕吐也不觉得苦不堪言。嘴馋的人可以忘却痛苦，饥饿贫困的人必定不重视性命。可以忘却痛苦的人，无论什么事情都可以欺瞒；不怕死的人，无论什么事情都敢做。因此，君主将自己的欲望与百姓的欲望协调一致，将自己的饥饱与百姓的饥饱协调一致。君主愤怒就是百姓愤怒，君主抱怨是百姓抱怨。能够懂得这个道理，天下哪里还会有叛乱呢？

---

①燔骨：炙肉中的骨头。
②醇酎：重酿之醇酒。
③哕：呕吐。

Bones of Roasted Meat

Those who gnaw on the bones of roasted meat do not feel pain even if their lips and tongues are blistered; those who drink wine do not feel the pain even if they drink till they vomit. He who has a gluttonous appetite can forget his pain in eating food, and he who is hungry and poor certainly do not value his life. He who can forget pain can deceive in whatever he does, and he who is not afraid of death can risk to do anything. Therefore, the monarch compares his desires with the desires of the people, and his hunger and satiety with the hunger and satiety of the people. Then the ruler's anger is the people's anger, and the ruler's complaint is the people's complaint. How could there be rebellion in the world if one can understand this?

化书之 85

·原文·

食 迷

民有嗜食而饱死者，有婪食而鲠①死者，有感食而义死者，有辱食而愤死者，有争食而斗死者，人或笑之。殊不知官所以务禄，禄所以务食；贾所以务财，财所以务食。而官以矫佞馋谳②而律死者，贾以波涛江海而溺死者，而不知所务之端，不知得死之由，而迁怨于辈流③，归咎于江海，食之迷也。

·白话·

食 迷

有贪吃而被撑死的，有暴食而被噎死的，有因食物所感动赴义而死的，有因食物受辱而气愤致死的，有为争夺食物斗殴而死的，对此众人或许会嗤之一笑。殊不知当官的之所以追求俸禄，是因为俸禄可以换来美食；商人之所以追求钱财，是因为钱财可以换来美食。当官的因奸佞谗言诽谤而依照刑律处死，经商的因船沉江海而溺死，至死不知所追求的事情是什么，不知为何而死的原因是什么，因而当官的将原因迁怒于同僚的排挤迫害，经商的将原因归咎于波涛无常，这都是陷于饮食的

---

①鲠：食骨留咽喉中，或作堵塞。
②谳：诽谤，谤言。
③辈流：同辈人。

迷惑中而已。

Chapter 85

Addiction to Food

There are gluttons who are stuffed to death ;there are people who eat too much and and choke to death; there are righteous people who die for food; there are people who are insulted because of food and die of indignation; there are people who fight for food and die for it. Some people may laugh at all these. But what people do not know is that the officials pursue high salary, because the salary can be exchanged for food; businessmen pursue money, because money can be exchanged for food. Due to slanders, the officials are executed according to the law, and the businessmen are drowned due to the sinking of ships. Till their death, they do not know what on earth they pursue and for what they die. Therefore, the officials attribute their unfair treatment to the slander of other officials, and the businessmen blame the the unpredictability of rivers and oceans for their misfortunes. In fact, they are all under the spell of food.

化书之**86**

战 欲

食之欲也，思盐梅①之状，则辄有所咽而不能禁；见盘肴之盛，则若所吞而不能遏。饥思啖牛，渴思饮海。故欲之于人也如贼，人之于欲也如战。当战之际，锦绣珠玉不足为富，冠冕旌旗不足为贵，金石丝竹②不闻其音，宫室台榭不见其丽。况民复常馁，民情常迫，而论以仁义，其可信乎？讲以刑政，其可畏乎？

战 欲

食欲，是一想到盐制梅子，就会忍不住的咽口水；一看见盘中美食，也会忍不住咽口水。饥饿的时候想要有像一头牛那么多的东西来吃，干渴的时候想要有像大海一样多的水来喝。因此，欲望对于人来说就像是贼，而人对于欲望来说就像是士兵面临战争。在战争中，对战斗的人来说即使拥有锦绣珠玉不算富有，即使佩有冠冕旌旗也不为尊贵，即使乐器演奏也听不到声音，即使面对宫室台榭也看不见它的瑰丽。更何况百姓常常处于饥饿状态，百姓的处境往往很窘迫，用仁义说教，有谁

①盐梅：即酸梅。
②金石丝竹：指代乐器。金石，钟磬之类。

会相信呢？用刑罚政令威胁，有谁会害怕呢？

Chapter 86

Fight Against Appetite

　　You can't help your mouth watering at the thought of salted plums; you can't help but swallow at the sight of a plate of delicacies, and these are all caused by your appetite. When you are hungry, you want to have as much as a cow to eat, and when you are thirsty, you want to have as much water to drink as the ocean. Therefore, appetite is like a thief to man,while man is like a soldier ready to fight to appetite. To a soldier during a war, even the possession of embroidery and jewels is not considered rich, even the wearing of a crown is not honored, even the sound of musical instruments is not heard, and even the splendor of palaces is not seen. What's more, the people were often in a state of hunger and in dire conditions. Who would believe in the preaching of benevolence and righteousness? Who would be afraid if they were threatened with punishment and decrees?

化书之 **87**

原文

胶　竿

执胶竿捕黄雀，黄雀从而噪之；捧盘食享乌鸟①，乌鸟从而告之。是知至暴者无所不异，至食者无所不同。故蛇豕②可以友而群，虎兕③可以狎④而驯，四夷⑤可以率而宾。异族犹若此，况复人⑥之人。

白话

胶　竿

手执粘胶长竿捕捉黄雀，黄雀惊叫着躲避；手捧盛着食物的盘子喂乌鸦，乌鸦跟随着并奔走相告。于是可以知道，遇到暴行时，都会存在异心；看到食物时，反应则都相同。因此，用食物的方法，毒蛇野猪也可以与我友好的相处，猛虎也可以与我游戏并被驯服，不开化的落后民族也可以向我臣服。不同类的动物和其他的民族都可以这样，更何况我们自己民族的人呢？

---

① 乌鸟：乌鸦。

② 蛇豕：猪和蛇。

③ 兕：兽名。古书中常拿兕和犀对举。《尔雅释兽》认为兕似牛，犀似猪。

④ 狎：亲近，亲密。

⑤ 四夷：东夷、西戎、南蛮、北狄，旧时统称四夷。是古代对华夏族以外各族的泛称。

⑥ 复人：同类之人。

Chapter 87

Sticky Poles

When one holds a long sticky pole in one's hand to catch siskins, they shriek at him; when one holds a plate with food in one's hand to feed crows, they follow him and fly to tell each other. Thus it is known that when violence is used, there will be a rebellion, but when food is used, the crowd will follow. Therefore, if the world is ruled with food, even the poisonous snakes and wild boars can be friendly with the rulers, even the tigers can be tamed and hang around with the rulers, and even the uncivilized and backward nations can submit to the rulers. Different animals and other nations will act like this, let alone our own people!

化书之 **88**

庚 辛

　　庚氏穴池，构竹为凭槛，登之者其声"策策"^①焉。辛氏穴池，构木为凭槛，登之者其"堂堂"^②焉。二氏俱牧鱼于池中，每凭槛投饥，鱼必踊跃而出。他日但闻"策策""堂堂"之声，不投饵亦踊跃而出，则是庚氏之鱼可名"策策"，辛氏之鱼可名"堂堂"，食之化也。

庚 辛

　　庚姓人家挖掘池塘，用竹子做成栅栏和踏板，踩踏上去发出"策策"的声音；辛姓人家挖掘池塘，用木头做成栅栏和踏板，踩踏上去发出"堂堂"的声音。两户人家都在池塘中养鱼，每次到栅栏边上去投饵料，鱼儿必定踊跃而出。以后只要听到"策策""堂堂"之声，不投饵鱼儿也会踊跃而出，则是庚氏养的鱼可以叫做"策策"，辛氏养的鱼可以叫做"堂堂"。这就是用食物教化的结果。

---

①策策：象声词。
②堂堂：象声词。

Chapter 88

The Family of Geng and Xin

The family of Geng excavated a pond for fish farming. The fence and deck around the pond are made of bamboo, and every time they step on the deck and come close to the fence, there comes the sound of "ce ce[1]..." The family of Xin also excavated a pond for fish farming. The fence and deck around the pond are made of wood, and every time they step on the deck and come close to the fence, there comes the sound of "tang tang...".

Every time the two families come near the fence to feed the fish, they jump out of water to fight for the food. As long as they hear the sound of "ce ce" "tang tang", they will jump out of water enthusiastically even when there is no food.The fish of Geng can be called "Ce Ce", and the fish of Xin can be called "Tang Tang". This is the result of indoctrination with food.

①Ce Ce ...Tang Tang ...: These two are onomatopoeia.

化书之**89**

·原文·

兴 亡

疮者人之痛，火者人之急，而民喻饥谓之疮，比饿谓之火，盖情有所切也。夫鲍鱼[①]与腐尸无异，鲼鲽[②]与足垢无殊，而人常食之。饱犹若是，饥则可知。苟其饥也，无所不食，苟其迫也，无所不为。斯所以为兴亡之机。

·白话·

兴 亡

疮是人身上的痛苦，火是令人着急的事情，而百姓将饥比喻为疮，将饿比喻为火，都是因为有切身体会。腌制的咸鱼与腐烂的尸体一样，鱼鳔和鱼肠腌制成的酱与脚上的污垢没有什么差别，而人们常常吃这种东西。饱的时候就已经这样了，就可以知道饥饿的时候是什么样子了。如果到了饥饿的时候，什么东西都敢吃，如果到了被逼无奈的时候，什么事情都敢做。所以，这就是关乎国家兴亡的关键所在。

[①]鲍鱼：湿的腌鱼，味腥臭。
[②]鲼鲽（zhú yí）：鱼鳔、鱼肠用盐或蜜渍成的酱。

Chapter 89

Rise and Fall

A sore is a pain in a person's body, and fire is something that causes anxiety. The people compare hunger to sores and fire because it is just as painful to them. The smell of pickled fish is the same as that of a decaying corpse, and there is no difference in the taste of fish sauce① and that of the dirt on the foot, and the people often eat such things. It is already like this when you are full, so you can know what it is like when you are hungry. If one is starving to death, he will dare to eat anything, and if one is forced to the corner, he will risk to do anything. So, this is the key to the rise and fall of a country.

---

①fish sauce: Fish bladder and fish intestines are salted or honeyed to make a sauce.

化书之 **90**

·原文·

雀 鼠

人所以恶雀鼠^①者，谓其有攘^②窃之行；雀鼠所以疑人者，谓其怀盗贼之心。夫上以食而辱下，下以食而欺上，上不得不恶下，下不得不疑上，各有所切也。夫剜其肌、啖其肉，不得不哭；扼其喉、夺其哺，不得不怒。民之瘠也由剜其肌，民之馁也由夺其哺。呜呼，惜哉！

·白话·

雀 鼠

人们之所以憎恶老鼠麻雀，是因为它们有偷窃行为；老鼠和麻雀之所以不相信人类，是因为人类有抢劫偷盗之心。朝廷用食物而欺辱百姓，百姓的人们用食物而欺骗朝廷。朝廷不得不憎恶百姓，百姓不得不疑心朝廷，各有所关心的事情。用刀剜人们的筋骨，吃人们的肉，人们不得不哭号；扼住人们的咽喉，抢夺人们的食物，人们不得不愤怒。百姓的贫瘠就像被剜了筋骨，百姓的饥饿就像被夺了食物。真令人叹息啊。

① 雀鼠：麻雀和老鼠。
② 攘：偷窃。

Chapter 90

Sparrows and Rats

The reason why people hate sparrows and rats is that they think they are thieves; the reason why sparrows and rats do not trust people is that they think people intend to rob and steal. The upper class bullies the lower class with food, and the people of the lower class deceive the upper class with food. The upper class naturally hate the lower class, while the lower class are naturally suspicious of the upper class, and each had something to care about. With their sinews being plucked out and their flesh being eaten, people will definitely cry; with their throats being choked and their food being robbed, people will definitely be angry. The poverty of the people was like having their sinews and bones plucked out, and the hunger of the people was like having their food taken away. What a pity!

化书之 **91**

· 原文 ·

无 为

牛可使之驾，马可使之负，犬可使之守，鹰可使之击，盖食有所感也。猕猴①可使之舞，鹦鹉可使之语，鸥鸢②可使之死斗，蝼蚁可使之合战，盖食有所教也。鱼可使之吞钩，虎可使之入陷，雁可使之触纲，敌国可使之自援，盖食有所利也，天地可使之交泰③，神明可使之掖卫④，高尚可使之屈折⑤，夷狄⑥可使之委伏⑦，盖食有所奉也。故自天子至于庶人，暨乎万族，皆可以食而通之。我服布素⑧则民自暖，我食葵藿⑨则民自饱。善用其道者，可以肩无为之化。

①猕猴：猴之一种，面部红色无毛，尾短。四肢均像人手。
②鸥鸢：即鸥鸟/也作鹞鹰。
③交泰：指天地之气融合贯通，生养万物。
④掖卫：掖，扶持，导引；卫，守卫。
⑤屈折：折服，屈卑。
⑥夷狄：古代对周边民族的泛称。
⑦委伏：委顺臣服。
⑧布素：布质朴素的衣服。
⑨葵藿：野菜名。

· 白话 ·

无　为

可以让牛来拉车，可以让马来驮物，可以让狗来看家，可以让鹰来捕猎，这都是食物对这些动物所产生的感化。可以让猕猴舞蹈，可以让鹦鹉说话，可以让鸥鸢死斗，可以让蝼蚁交战，都是用食物训练出来的。可以让鱼吞钩，可以让老虎掉入陷井，可以让大雁触上罗网，可以让敌国自己牵制自己，都是食物可以利用的方面。可以让天地交融，可以让神明来护卫，可以让高尚的人屈折，可以让蛮夷之族降伏，都是食物获得尊奉的原因吧。因此上至天子下至百姓，甚至于所有生灵族类，都可以用食物来沟通。君主穿着粗布衣服，则百姓自然就有御寒衣物，君主以野菜为食物，则百姓自然无饥饿之忧。善于按照衣食之需这样的道理管理的，就可以肩负起用无为来教化百姓的重任。

Chapter 91

Wuwei[1]

One can make an ox pull a cart, a horse carry things, a dog watch the house, and an eagle hunt, because these animals are all motivated by food. The macaque can be made to dance, the parrot can be made to talk, the owl can be made to fight, and the ant can be made to start a war, because they are all trained with food. The fish may swallow the hook, the tiger may fall into the trap, the wild geese may throw themselves into the net, and the

---

[1]Wuwei: The practice of taking no action that is not in accord with the natural course of the universe.

enemies may shoot themselves in the foot, and these are profitable aspects of food. Heaven and earth can be made to communicate, gods can be asked to guard people, noble people can be made humble, barbarian tribes can be made submissive, and these are why food is worshiped. Therefore, from the emperor to the people, and even all living creatures, all people can communicate with food. If the ruler wears coarse clothes, the people will naturally have warm clothes, and if the ruler uses Kui and Huo[1] as food, the people will naturally be free from hunger. Those who are good at managing things in accordance with the needs of food and clothing can take on the important task of educating the people with Wuwei.

---

[1]Kui and Huo: It refers to some of the important vegetables in ancient times. Huo is the leaf of soybeen. Kui and Huo refer to crude food.

王　者

　　猎食者母，分乳者子。全生者子，触纲者母。母不知子之所累，子不知母之所苦。王者衣缨①之费、盘肴之直②，岁不过乎百万，而封人之土地，与人之富贵，百万之百万。如咂③王之肌，如饮王之血。乐在于下，怨在于上，利归于众，咎归于王。夫不自贵，天下安敢贵？不自富，天下安敢富？

王　者

　　捕猎食物的是母亲，分享食物的是孩子。遇到危险，逃生的是孩子，撞到猎网的是母亲。母亲并不觉得是受到孩子的拖累，孩子并不知道母亲受到的苦难。君王用于服饰和饮食上面的花费，一年下来不过百万，而分给他人的土地、赏给他人的财富，价值是君王每年花费的百万倍。这就像吃君王的肉，喝君王的血。欢欣喜悦的是众人，受到抱怨的是君王，利益归于众人，罪责归于君王。因此，若君王自己不得到尊贵，天下谁敢得到尊贵？君王自己不富足，天下谁敢富足？

---

①缨：结冠的带子。

②直：通"值"。

③咂：吮吸。

Chapter 92

The King

It is the mothers who hunt for food, and it is the children who share the food. In case of danger, it is the children who escape, and it is the mothers who are there to protect their children. The mothers do not feel that they are dragged down by their children, and the children do not know the sufferings of their mothers. The emperor spends only a million dollars a year on clothing and food, but the land given to others and the wealth rewarded to others are worth a million times more than the emperor spends each year. This is like eating the emperor's flesh and drinking the emperor's blood. It is the people who rejoice, but it is the emperor who gets complained, and the benefits go to the people while the guilt to the emperor. Therefore, if the emperor himself is not honored, who in the world will dare to be honored? If the emperor himself is not rich, who in the world will dare to be rich?

鸱鸢

有智者悯鸱鸢[1]之击腐鼠，嗟蝼蚁之驾毙虫，谓其为虫不若为人。殊不知当歉岁则争臭毙之尸，值严围[2]则食父子之肉。斯豺狼之所不忍为，而人为之，则其为人不若为虫。是知君无食必不仁，臣无食必不义，士无食必不礼，民无食必不智，万类无食必不信。是以食为五常之本，五常为食之末。苟王者能均其衣，能让其食，则黔黎[3]相悦，仁之至也；父子相爱，义之至也；饥饱相让，礼之至也；进退相得，智之至也；许诺相从，信之至也。教之善也在于食，教之不善也在于食。其物甚卑，其用甚尊；其名尤细，其化尤大。是谓无价之宝。

鸱鸢

聪明的人为那些以腐烂老鼠为食物的鹰隼而感到怜悯，为那些运送死掉的虫子

---

① 鸱鸢：鸱鸟，也是鹞鹰。
② 严围：用兵守城的危险时刻。
③ 黔黎：黔首、黎民的合称，即庶民、百姓。

为食物的蝼蚁叹息，感叹到做虫子真是不如做人啊。殊不知人类在歉收年景也有争夺发臭的死尸为食的情况，在严寒围困境况下也有父与子相食的情况。连豺狼也不忍心做的事情而人类却可以做，从这点上看做人还不如做虫子啊。于是可以知道，君主没有食物的情况下必然会残暴，大臣没有食物的情况下必然会邪恶，士大夫阶层没有食物的情况下必然粗野，百姓没有食物的情况下必然会愚昧，不论哪种民族在没有食物的情况下必然没有诚信可言。因此，食物是仁义礼智信这五常的根本，而五常则只是食物的末梢。若君王能够均让出衣物和食物，则百姓就会由衷喜悦，这就有了仁爱；父子相互爱护，就有了义气；人们在饥饿的时候相互谦让，就有了礼节；随着情况变化进退有据，就有了智慧；做出许诺并兑现许诺，就有了诚信。教化百姓的好处在于食物，教化百姓不好的地方也在于食物。食物作为东西来说甚为卑贱，但是其作用来说甚为尊贵；食物的名字很细微，但是在万物演化过程中的作用很大，可以称作无价之宝了。

Chapter 93

Sparrow Hawks

The smart people feel pity for the sparrow hawks who feed on rotting mice, and sigh for the ants who transport dead bugs for food, lamenting that it is better to be a human than a bug. What they do not know is that human beings in a bad harvest year also have to compete for the stinking corpse as food, in bitterly cold climate there are also fathers and sons who eat each other for food. Human beings can do things that even jackals cannot bear to do, and from this point of view, to be a bug is better than to be a human. Thus, it is known that a monarch without food is bound to be brutal, a minister without food is bound to be wicked, the official class without food are bound to be rude, a person without food is

bound to be ignorant, and there is definitely no integrity whatever nation it is if it has no food. Therefore, food is the root of the Five Virtues of Benevolence, Righteousness, Ritual, Wisdom and Faithfulness, while the Five Virtues are only the end branches of food. If an emperor can give up some of their clothes and food to common people, the people will be happy from the bottom of their hearts, and there comes Benevolence; if fathers and sons can love and protect each other, then there comes Righteousness; if people can give up food to share with others when they are hungry, then there comes Ritual; if people can be flexible with the changing situation, then there comes Wisdom; if people can make promises and keep them, then there comes Faithfulness. What is good about educating the people is food, however, what is bad about educating the people is also food. Food, if only being regarded as an object, is inexpensive. However, if we view food from the the function of it, it becomes valuable. The role food plays in the evolution of all things is so great that it can be called a priceless object.

卷 六
Volume 6

俭 化

The Transformation of Frugality

化书之 **94**

太 平

　　夫水火，常用之物，用之不得其道，以至于败家，盖失于不简也。饮馔，常食之物，食之不得其道，以至于亡身，盖失于不节也。夫礼失于奢，乐失于淫。奢淫若水，去不复返，议欲救之，莫过乎俭。俭者，均食之道也。食均则仁义生，仁义生则礼乐序，礼乐序则民不怨，民不怨则神不怒，太平之业也。

太 平

　　水和火这两样东西，是人们生活中常常用到的，用的不对，就会毁灭家园，原因在于使用方法的过于繁杂。饮食是人们常常吃的东西，吃的不对，就会导致死亡，原因在于饮食方面没有节制。礼节若是过于繁琐就错了，音乐若是毫无节制便错了。繁琐和过度就像水一样，一去不复返，若要挽救，最好的方法就是节俭。节俭，就是每个人都获得同样的食物。食均自然就会产生仁义，有了仁义自然礼乐就会有序，礼乐有序百姓自然就没有抱怨，百姓不抱怨自然就不会引起天神发怒，这就是太平盛世。

Chapter 94

Peace

Water and fire are two things that people often use in life, but if people do not use them properly, they will destroy their houses, and the reason is that the method of using them is made too complicated. Food is something people eat daily, but if they do not eat appropriately, it will lead to death, and the reason is that there is no moderation in their diet. If the etiquette is too cumbersome, there must be something wrong with the etiquette. If the music is excessive, there must be something wrong with the music. This excessiveness is like water that never returns, and if one determines to fix them, the best way is to be frugal. Frugality means that everyone gets the same amount of food. With the same amount of food, there will be benevolence and righteousness, and with benevolence and righteousness, there will be orderly rituals and music, and with orderly rituals and music, there will not be any complaints from the people, and if the people do not complain, there will be no anger from the gods. Thereafter the world will be peaceful and prosperous.

化书之 95

权　衡①

服絺綌②者不寒，而衣之布帛③愈寒；食藜藿者不饥，而饭之黍稷④愈饥。是故我之情也，不可不虑；民之心也，不可不防。凡民之心，见负石者则乐于负涂⑤，见负涂者则乐于负薥⑥。饥寒无实状，轻重无必然，皆丰俭相形，彼我相平，我心重则民心重，我负轻则民负轻。能至于俭者，可以与民为权衡。

权　衡

穿粗布衣服的人不感到寒冷，穿绸缎衣服的人就越是感到寒冷；吃粗茶淡饭的人不感到饥饿，吃美食佳肴的人就越是感到饥饿。因此，君主的感受，不可不虑；而百姓的私心，不可不防。一般情况下老百姓的心理，见到别人背着石头，对自己

---

① 权衡：称量物体轻重的工具。权，称锤；衡，称杆。权衡在这里泛指权力。
② 絺綌：絺指细葛布，綌指粗葛布。两者都是将葛经过浸渍煮沦的加工法制成的。这里絺綌，指葛布衣服。这里泛指比较粗俗、朴素的衣服。
③ 布帛：丝、麻及棉织物的总称。这里泛指比较价值比较高的，比较高档的衣服。
④ 黍稷：泛指五谷杂粮。
⑤ 涂：泥
⑥ 薥：同"刍"。刍，饲草，草杆，草把。

背着泥土就没有怨言，见到别人背着泥土，对自己背着饲草就没有怨言。饥饿或寒冷没有用来判别的实实在在的标准，轻与重也没有必然或绝对的说法，都是由丰富与节俭相互比较，别人与自己相互比较而定。因此，自己的心里看重的，百姓的心里必然也是看重的，自己负担轻的百姓负担也就轻。能够用节俭来约束自己的，就可以胜任百姓的长官。

Chapter 95

Power

Those who wear coarse clothes do not feel cold, but those who wear satin clothes may feel cold; those who eat coarse food do not feel hungry, but those who eat good food may feel hungry. Therefore, the ruler cannot ignore his own feelings, nor can he neglect people's thoughts. It is the general psychology of the people that when they see others carrying stones, they will stop complaining about themselves carrying clay, and when they see others carrying clay, they will stop complaining about themselves carrying hay. There is no universal criterion for judging hunger or coldness, and there is no absolute standard about lightness and heaviness, which are all determined through comparison and contrast—comparing abundance with frugality, and comparing others with themselves. Therefore, what one values must also be valued by the people, and the people's burden will be light if the governor's burden is light. He who is able to discipline himself with frugality can be a competent governor of the people.

·原文·

礼　道

礼贵于盛，俭贵于不盛；礼贵于备，俭贵于不备；礼贵于簪绂①，俭贵于布素；礼贵于炳焕②，俭贵于寂寞。富而富之愈不乐，贵而贵之愈不美，赏而赏之愈不足，爱而爱之愈不敬。金玉者，富之常；官爵者，贵之常。渴饮则甘，饥食则香。夫惟俭，所以能知非常。

·白话·

礼　道

对礼节来说，最注重隆重，对节俭来说，关键是不能隆重；对于礼节来说最注重的是完备，面面俱到，对于节俭来说最注重的是不完备，不能面面俱到；对于礼节来说服饰华贵特别重要，对于节俭来说，衣着朴素特别重要；对于礼节来说最注重的是高调、鲜明、华丽，对于节俭来说最注重的是低调、清静、恬淡。越来越富裕却更不快乐，越来越显贵却觉得觉得不美满，受到的赏赐越来越多却不满足，受到的爱戴越来越多却仍觉得不受尊敬。金银珠玉对富人来说习以为常，高官厚禄对

① 簪绂：簪，冠簪；绂，丝制之缨带。皆古礼服之制，以喻显贵。
② 炳焕：光明显耀。

地位尊贵的人来说习以为常。口渴的时候饮水就会觉得甘美，饥饿的时候吃东西就会觉得香甜。因此，只有节俭，才能够品味事物的珍贵。

Chapter 96

Etiquette

To etiquette, it is important to be grand, while frugality requires it not to be grand; to etiquette, it is important to be complete, while frugality requires it not to be so complete; to etiquette, it is important to wear gorgeous official clothes, while frugality requires one to wear rough clothes; to etiquette, it is important to be gorgeous and high-profile, while frugality requires one to be quiet and in low-profile. The richer you are the more you feel unhappy, the more prestigious you are the more you feel inefficient, the more rewards you receive the more you feel dissatisfied, the more respect you get the more you feel disrespected. Gold, silver, pearls and jade are commonplace for the rich, and big titles and high salaries are commonplace for those with honored status. The water tastes sweeter if you drink it when you are thirsty, and the food will taste more delicious if you eat them when you are hungry. Therefore, everything can be savored only when one is frugal.

化书之 97

食 象

观食象者食牛不足，观戴冕者戴冠不足。不足有所自，不廉有所始。是知王好奢则臣不足，臣好奢则士不足，士好奢则民不足，民好奢则天下不足。夫天下之物十之，王好一，民亦一；王好五，民亦五；王好十，民亦十。以十论之，则是十家为一家，十国为一国，十天下为一天下，何不弊之有！

食 象

看到吃大象的，就对自己吃牛感到不满足，看到戴王冕的，就对自己戴的官帽不满足。不满足的心理滋生，不廉洁的事情就开始了。于是可以知道，君王喜好奢侈，则下面大臣就会对自己的生活不满足；大臣喜好奢侈，则下面士大夫就会对自己的生活感到不满足；士大夫喜好奢侈，则下面百姓就会对自己的生活感到不满足；百姓喜好奢侈，则天下生产出来的东西就会发生匮缺。比如将天下的东西分为十种，若君王喜好其中一种，百姓也喜好一种；若君王喜好其中五种，百姓也喜好五种；若君王喜好十种，百姓也喜好十种。还是用十来比方，则是十家为一家，十国为一国，十个天下为一个天下，若是如此，怎会没有弊端呢？

Eating Elephants

When seeing other people eat the meat of the elephants, people will feel dissatisfied with themselves eating beef; when seeing other people wear a crown, people will not be satisfied with the official hat they themselves wear. When the thought of dissatisfaction comes to a person's mind, corruption appears. Therefore, you can find that when the emperor enjoys luxury, then the following ministers will be dissatisfied with their own lives; when ministers enjoy luxury, then the following scholars and officials will be dissatisfied with their own lives; when scholars and officials enjoy luxury, then the following people will be dissatisfied with their own lives; when the people enjoy luxury, then there will be shortage of products in the world. Suppose we divide the world into ten types of things. If the emperor prefers one of them, the people will also want one; if the emperor prefers five of them, the people will also want five; if the emperor prefers ten, the people will also want ten. Still using the analogy of ten, one can find that if ten families are regarded as one family, ten countries are regarded as one country, ten worlds are regarded as one world, there must be some drawbacks.

化书之 **98**

·原文·

民 情

其夫好饮酒者，其妻必贫。其子好臂鹰者，其家必困。剩养一仆，日饭三瓯①，岁计千瓯。以一岁计之，可享千兵。王者岁率是享，则必告劳而聚怨，病在于增不在于损。王驾牛车，民骄于行；王居士陛，民耻于平。杜之于渐，化之于俭。所以见葛藟②不足者，则乐然服布素之衣；见窳③杯而食者，则欣然用陶匏④之器，民之情也。

·白话·

民 情

丈夫好饮酒，妻子必然贫穷。孩子喜好架鹰隼的，家里必然困苦。家中多养一个仆人，每天需要三钵饭食，一年下来就是一千余钵饭食。按一年计算，就可以够千名兵士一餐。君王每年都率领许多这样的人消耗饭食，就必然会有人诉苦从而聚

---

① 瓯：盆盂。
② 葛藟：植物名。又称"千岁藟"。落叶本质藤本。茎皮纤维可织葛布，较为粗陋。
③ 窳：粗劣、不坚实。多指器物的质地。
④ 匏：匏瓜，俗叫瓢葫芦，葫芦的一种果实。陶匏即陶制的盆。

积民怨，其问题在于花费不减少反而增加。君王驾着牛车出行，百姓就会对自己步行自豪；君王居住豪宅，百姓就会为自己居住平常而羞愧。防范弊病要从微小的事情开始，最后转化落实到节俭上。看见穿着藤葛衣服的，就会对自己粗布衣服感到欣然，见到用粗劣器物来饮食的，就会对自己的陶器感到高兴。这就是民众的心理愿望。

Chapter 98

Public Sentiment

If a husband is a heavy drinker, his wife is bound to be poor. If child is fond of falcons, his family is bound to be poor. If you keep one more servant in your house, you need three more bowls of food per day, which is more than a thousand bowls of food in one year, enough for one meal for a thousand soldiers. If the emperor has many people like this to consume food every year, there are bound to be complaints and public discontent, and what goes wrong here lies in the increase of expenses rather than in its decrease. If the emperor travels in an oxcart, the people will be proud of walking; if the emperor lives in a luxurious mansion, the people will be ashamed of living in an ordinary house. The prevention of ills should start from the smallest things, and finally frugality should be advocated and implemented. When you see one wearing clothes made of ko-hemp cloth, you will be pleased with your coarse linen clothes; when you see one eating with coarse and inferior utensils, you will be pleased with your pottery utensils. This is the sentiment of the people.

·原文·

悭 号

世有悭①号者，人以为大辱，殊不知始得为纯俭之道也。于己无所与，于民无所取。我耕我食，我蚕我衣。妻子②不寒，婢仆不饥。人不怨之，神不罪之。故一人知俭则一家富，王者知俭则天下富。

·白话·

悭 号

世上有人外号吝啬鬼，人们都以为对他是很大的侮辱，殊不知他已经得到纯正的节俭之道。对自己一无所给，对他人一无所求。自己耕作自己获取饭食，自己养蚕自己织布穿衣。妻子和孩子有衣服穿不会寒冷，仆人婢女有饭食不会饥饿。别人不对他抱怨，神仙不对他降罪。因此可知，一人懂得节俭则一家富裕，君王懂得节俭则天下富裕。

①悭：吝啬。悭号者，即绰号叫吝啬鬼的人。
②妻子：妻子和孩子。

The Nicknamed Miser

When someone in the world is nicknamed "miser," people think it is a great insult to him, but what they do not know is that he has got the key to frugality. He gives nothing to himself and asks nothing from others. He cultivates his own land and harvests his own food, raises his own silkworms and weaves his own clothes. His wife and children have clothes to wear and do not get cold, and his servants and maids have food and do not go hungry. Others do not complain against him, and the gods do not condemn him. Therefore, it is clear that if one person knows how to be frugal, a family will be rich, and if an emperor knows how to be frugal, the whole world will be rich.

化书之 **100**

君 民

君之于民，异名而同爱。君乐驰骋，民亦乐之；君喜声色，民亦喜之；君好珠玉，民亦好之；君嗜滋味，民亦嗜之。其名则异，其爱则同。所以服布素者，爱士之簪组[1]；服士之簪组者，爱公卿之剑佩；服公卿之剑佩者，爱王者之旒冕[2]，是故王者居兆民所爱之地，不得不虑也。况金根玉辂[3]夺其货，高台崇榭夺其力，是贾[4]民之怨，是教民之爱。所以积薪聚米，一岁之计，而易金换玉，一日之费，不得不困，不得不俭。

君 民

君王和百姓，称谓不同而爱好是相同的。君王喜好骑马，百姓也喜欢骑马；君王喜好曲乐美色，百姓也喜欢曲乐美色；君王喜好珍珠宝玉，百姓也喜欢珍珠宝玉；

---

[1] 簪组：簪，冠簪；组，冠带。指官服之显贵。
[2] 旒冕：旒，冕冠前悬垂的玉串。
[3] 辂：大车。
[4] 贾：招致，谋求。

君王喜好美食，百姓也喜欢美食。人们的名声和地位不同而爱好相同。所以穿粗布衣服的，喜欢士大夫的冠簪和冠带；穿有冠簪和冠带衣服的，喜欢王公大臣的佩剑；穿有佩剑衣服的，喜欢君王戴的王冠。因此君王是处于全民所最倾慕的地位，不得不多虑。况且君王的金银器物和宝玉装饰的车驾是靠掠夺百姓财物获得的，楼台殿宇是靠驱使百姓力量建成的，这是在招致百姓的怨恨，也是在教百姓产生爱好。积聚柴薪米粮可以维持百姓一年生计，而将这些柴薪米粮换成金银珠玉，只够一天的花费，所以要想治理国家，不得不困苦，不得不节俭。

Chapter 100

The Emperor and the People

The emperor and the people have different status but the same hobbies. The emperor likes to ride horses, and the people also like to ride horses; the emperor likes music and beauties, and the people also like music and beauties; the emperor likes pearls and precious stones, and the people also like pearls and precious stones; the emperor likes delicacies, and the people also like delicacies. Their status are different but the preferences are the same. Therefore, those who wear coarse clothes all admire the crown pins and crown belts of the scholars and officials; those who wear clothes with crown pins and crown belts admire the swords of the emperor and ministers; those who wear clothes with swords admire the crown worn by the emperor. Therefore, the emperor is in the position that all people aspire for, and he has to be aware of it. Moreover, the emperor's gold, silver, and jade which decorate carriages are obtained by plundering the people's property, and the buildings and temples were built by gathering people's labor, thus incurring the people's resentment but also leading them to admire these luxuries. The accumulation of firewood and rice could sustain the people for a year, but if these firewood and rice were exchanged for gold, silver, pearls and jade, it would only be enough for one day's expenses, so the rulers should live on a tight budget and be frugal.

化书之 101

·原文·

乳 童

　　乳童拱手，谁敢戏之，岂在乎黼黻①也。牧竖②折腰，谁敢背③之，岂在乎刑政也。有宾主之敬，则鸡黍可以为大享④，岂在乎箫韶⑤也。有柔淑之态，则荆苎⑥可以行妇道，岂在乎组绣⑦也。而王者之制，设沟隍⑧以御之，陈棨戟⑨以卫之，蓄粟帛以养之，张栏槛以远之。盖有机于民，不得不藏；有私于己，不得不防。夫能张俭之机，民自不欺；用俭之私，我自不疑。夫俭者，可以为大人之师。

①黼黻：古代礼服上绣的半黑半白的花纹。
②竖：童仆。
③背：以背向之。
④大享：即大飨，大张筵宴。
⑤箫韶：相传舜之乐名。
⑥荆苎：荆，灌木名，种类甚多；苎，植物名，麻属。荆苎，旧时自称其妻。以荆枝为髻钗，用麻布制衣裙，为贫家妇女的装束。
⑦组绣：组．丝带；绣．绘画设色，五彩具备。此指华丽衣服。
⑧沟隍：沟，城堑；隍，无水的城壕。
⑨棨戟：棨，有缯衣的戟，为官吏出行的仪仗之一。棨戟，有缯衣或油漆的木戟，用为官吏出行时前导的仪仗。

乳　童

儿童向人拱手行礼，没有人敢去戏弄他，更不在乎幼童是否穿着华美衣服。牧童躬身施礼，没有人敢不理不睬转身就走，更不在乎刑罚以及各项政令是怎样规定的。有了宾主礼仪的尊敬，即使仅仅以谷物和鸡肉为食物也可以成为盛宴，更不在乎是否有伴舞伴歌。有了柔美贤淑的气质，则即使身上穿着粗布衣服也可以胜任为人之妇的本分，更不在乎是否有华丽的衣服。然而君王设立的制度，环城挖沟壕来防御百姓，装备军队来护卫自己，积蓄米粮布帛来养军队，设栅栏将自己和百姓远远的隔绝开来。这些设置都因为君王对百姓使用了计谋，因而不得不把自己藏起来；因为君王是为了自己的私心，因而不得不对百姓采取防御。如果能将计谋用于节俭，就不用担心百姓的不平；如果能对自己节俭，就不用怀疑他人。因此，节俭的人可以作为官员们的楷模。

Chapter 101

Children

When a child curtsies, no one dares to tease him, not caring whether the youngster is wearing fancy clothes or not. When a shepherd boy bows, no one dares to ignore him and turn away, and no one cares what the punishment and the decrees are. With the respect of the guest and the host, even if the food is only grain and chicken, it can be a feast with or without the company of dancing and singing. If a woman have the temperament of beauty and virtuousness, she is a competent woman even if she is wearing coarse clothes and

doesn't have any fancy clothes. However, the emperor sets up a system in which he orders his army to dig trenches around the city for defense against the people, equips his army for protection of himself, stores up rice, grain, and cloth to feed his army, and sets up a fence to separate himself from the people. All these systems are set up because the emperor has to hide himself from the people for secretly scheming against them, and because the emperor has to guard against the people for his own pwrposes. If he can practice the key of frugality, he does not have to worry about the people's loyalty; and if he can be thrifty with himself, he does not have to suspect others. Therefore, a frugal emperor can serve as a model for the officials.

化书之 102

·原文·

化　柄

俭于听可以养虚，俭于视可以养神，俭于言可以养气，俭于私可以护富，俭于公可以保贵，俭于门闼可以无盗贼，俭于环卫可以无叛乱，俭于职官可以无奸佞，俭于嫔嫱可以保寿命，俭于心可以出生死。是知俭可以为万化之柄。

·白话·

化　柄

节省用于听的精力可以涵养空虚之性，节省用于看的精力可以涵养意识，节省用于说话的精力可以涵养生命元气，节俭用于自己可以富足，节俭用于公事可以保障声誉，节俭用于自家门庭可以免除盗贼光顾，节俭用于安全护卫可以免除叛乱祸患，节俭用于官场可以避免奸佞之人，节俭用于内室可以延年益寿，节俭用于心里可以跳出生死。因此得知，节俭是控制所有变化的根本所在。

Chapter **102**

The Root of Transformation

Frugality in listening can cultivate one's nature of emptiness; frugality in seeing can nourish the consciousness; frugality in speaking can nourish Yuanqi; frugality in oneself can make one rich; frugality in dealing public affairs can protect one's reputation; frugality in one's own house can prevent the visit of thieves; frugality in security can prevent rebellion; frugality in officialdom can avoid treacherous people; frugality in sex can prolong life, and frugality in the heart can make one go beyond of life and death. Therefore, it can be known that frugality is the root of controlling all changes.

化书之 **103**

· 原文 ·

御　一

　　王者皆知御^①一可以治天下也，而不知孰谓之一。夫万道皆有一^②：仁亦有一，义亦有一，礼亦有一，智亦有一，信亦有一。一能贯五，五能宗一。能得一者，天下可以治。其道盖简而出自简之，其言非玄而人自玄之。是故终迷其要，竟惑其妙。所以议守一之道，莫过乎俭；俭之所律，则仁不荡^③，义不乱，礼不奢，智不变，信不惑。故心有所主，而用有所本，用有所本而民有所赖。

· 白话 ·

御　一

　　君王都知道掌握了一，也就是掌握了事情的根本，就可以统治天下，但是君王都不知道什么才能算是一。各种事物中都包含有各自的一：仁亦有一，义亦有一，礼亦

---

①御：封建社会指上级对下级的治理，统治。

②一指天地间的大道。《抱朴子·地真篇》说："道起于一，其贵无偶，各居一处，以象天地人，故曰三一也。天得一以清，地得一以宁……仙经曰：子欲长生，守一当明。"又云："守一存真，乃能通神。"万物生于一，一生于道，故守一即可至于道。可见，守一即可入道，与道冥合，宇宙天地万物人我，打成一片，而复归于浑沌无我的境界。所以"守一"即守道。

③荡：放纵、放荡。

有一，智亦有一，信亦有一。一能贯穿仁义礼智信这五者，仁义礼智信这五者能综合成为一。能得到这个一的人，就可以成为统治天下的君王。其中的道理是很简单的，这个简单的道理不过是从更简单的事情中得出来的；用语言表达起来也并不玄奥，不过人们自己把它弄得玄奥无比。因此，人们终日陷于迷局想要找出其中的关键，并且被其中的奥妙所蛊惑无法自拔。所以要说起守一的道理，不过就是节俭的道理而已。在节俭的约束下，仁爱不放荡，正义公正，礼节简洁，智慧稳固，诚信坚定。因此，心里有了主见，管理就有了依据；管理有了依据，百姓就有了可以依靠的东西。

Chapter 103

Hold on to Tao

All kings know that if they can hold on to Tao, they can master the fundamentals of things and then rule the world. However, what they do not know is what Tao means in this world. Tao is contained in everything: Tao is in Benevolence, Tao is in Righteousness, Tao is in Ritual, Tao is in Wisdom, and Tao is also in Faithfulness. Tao can penetrate these Five Virtues—Benevolence, Righteousness, Ritual, Wisdom, and Faithfulness, and these Five Virtues can be integrated into one. The person who can obtain Tao can become the ruler of the world. The truth of this is very simple, but this simple truth is derived from simpler things; it is not esoteric in words, but people make it esoteric themselves. So people spend their days in a maze trying to find out the key to it, compelled by the mystery of it and unable extricate themselves. Simply speaking, the truth of holding on to Tao is just the truth of frugality. Under the discipline of frugality, Benevolence is moderate; Righteousness is fair; Ritual is simple; Wisdom is solid, and Faithfulness is firm. Therefore, when there is Tao in the heart, there is a rule for management; when there is a rule for management, the people have something to rely on.

化书之104

·原文·

三　皇

君俭则臣知足，臣俭则士知足，士俭则民知足，民俭则天下知足。天下知足，所以无贪财，无竞名，无奸蠹①，无欺罔，无矫佞。是故礼义自生，刑政自宁，沟垒自平，甲兵自停，游荡自耕，所以三皇②之化行。

·白话·

三　皇

君王节俭，则王公大臣就会知足；王公大臣节俭，则士大夫阶层就会知足；士大夫阶层节俭，则百姓就会知足；百姓节俭，天下就会知足。天下知足，所以就没有贪财，就没有争夺名誉地位，就没有奸佞和蠹虫，就没有欺上瞒下，就没有无理取闹和巧言谄媚。因而礼节和公正自然就产生出来，刑罚和政令自然就没有用处，用来隔离君王和百姓的沟壑自然就会被填平，军队自然就解散，游荡不定的人们自然就会从事耕作，所以三皇的教化自然就会推广流行。

①奸蠹：奸诈狡猾，邪恶不正直的人。
②三皇：传说中远古部落的酋长，其说不一，一般认为是伏羲、神农、燧人。

Chapter 104

Three Clan-rulers (Three Huang)[①]

If the emperor is frugal, the king and his ministers will be content; if the king and his ministers are frugal, the officials and scholars will be content; if the officials and scholars are frugal, the people will be content; if the people are frugal, the world will be content. If the world is content, there will neither be greed for money, competition for honorable positions, nor the need for treachery, deceitfulness, unreasonable, or flattering words. The ditch that separated the king from the people would be filled up, the army would be disbanded, and the wandering people would be engaged in farming, so that the moral cultivation of the time of the Three Clan-rulers would spread.

---

①Three Clan-rulers: it generally refers to Fuxi, Shennong and Suiren.They are all mythological figures in ancient times.

化书之 **105**

·原文·

天　牧^①

　　奢者三岁之计，一岁之用；俭者一岁之计，三岁之用。至奢者犹不及，至俭者尚有馀。奢者富不足，俭者贫有馀。奢者心常贫，俭者心常富。奢者好亲人，所以多过，俭者能远人，所以寡祸。奢者事君必有所辱，俭者事君必保其禄。奢者多忧，俭者多福，能终其俭者，可以为天下之牧。

·白话·

天　牧

　　奢侈的人可以支撑三年生活的花费，一年就用光了；节俭的人可以支撑一年的花费，支撑了三年。对奢侈的人来说不够用的，对节俭的人来说还有富余。奢侈的人虽然富裕但是总是不够用，节俭的人虽然贫穷但是总是有富余。奢侈的人心底常常是贫乏的，节俭的人心底常常是富足的。奢侈的人热衷与别人打交道，所以多有过失；节俭的人不热衷与别人打交道，所以能够远离祸患。奢侈的人为君王做事情必然会受到耻辱，节俭的人为君王做事情肯定会保障自己的俸禄。奢侈的人多忧，节俭的人多福。以节俭律己并能够坚持下来的人，就可以成为全天下的治理者。

①牧：管理。天牧在这里指天下的管理者。

Chapter 105

Rulers of the World

To an extravagant person, the money that can originally support him for three years of life will be used up by him within one year; to a frugal person, the money that can originally only support him for one year will be able to support him for three years. What is not enough for the extravagant person is surplus for the frugal person. The extravagant person is rich but is always unsatisfied; the frugal person is poor but always has a surplus. The heart of the extravagant man is often poor, and the heart of the frugal man is often rich. The extravagant man is eager to interact with others, so inevitably he may make many faults; the frugal man is not eager to interact with others, so he is able to keep away from misfortunes. The extravagant man who does things for the emperor is bound to be disgraced, and the frugal man who does things for the emperor is sure to secure his salary. Those who are extravagant have many worries, and those who are thrifty have many blessings. He who disciplines himself with frugality and is able to persevere, and can become the governor of the whole world.

·原文·

雕　笼

悬雕笼、事玉粒养黄雀，黄雀终不乐。垂礼乐、设赏罚教生民，生民终不泰。夫心不可安而自安之，道不可守而自守之，民不可化而自化之。所以俭于台榭则民力有馀，俭于宝货则民财有馀，俭于战伐则民时有馀。不与之由与之也，不取之由取之也。海伯亡鱼，不出于海；国君亡马，不出于国。

·白话·

雕　笼

悬挂精雕细琢的笼子，用珠玉一样的谷粒喂养黄雀，黄雀终日无欢。垂示礼乐制度，设置赏罚刑律来管理百姓，百姓终日心里不安泰。心不可以用外力安抚，而只可以靠自己安抚；道不可以用人来守护，而只可以靠自身来守护；百姓不可以用外力强行改变，而只可以靠自己改变。所以在建筑楼台亭榭上节俭，则百姓的物力就会有富余；在珠宝上节俭，则百姓的财力就会有富余；在征战上节俭，则百姓的时间就会有富余。不给就像给了一样，不拿就像拿了一样。就像海神丢失了鱼，丢失的鱼不会出了大海的范围；国君丢失了马，丢失的马不会出了国家的范围。

Chapter 106

The Cage with Fine Carvings

When the cage with fine carvings is hung and the yellow finches are fed with grain like pearls, the birds are joyless all day long. When the system of rituals and rewards and punishments are set to govern the people, the people will be restless all day long. The heart cannot be appeased by external forces, but only by themselves; Tao cannot be guarded by people, but only by oneself; the people cannot be forcibly changed by external forces, but only by oneself. Therefore, if one is thrifty in building palaces and pavilions, then the people will have a surplus of material resources; if one is thrifty in jewelry, then the people will have a surplus of financial resources; if one is thrifty in conquests, then the people will have a surplus of time. Even if you do not give anything, it is as if you have given many things, and even if you do not take anything, it is as if you have taken many things. When the god of the sea loses a fish, the lost fish will not go out of the range of the sea; when the king of the country loses a horse, the lost horse will not go out of the range of the country.

礼　要

　　夫礼者，道出于君而君由①不知，事出于职而职由不明。儒者棲山林②，敬师友，穷礼乐，讲本末。暨乎见羽葆③车辂之状，钟鼓箫韶④之作，则矍⑤然若鹿，怡然若豕；若醉于酒，若溺于水，莫知道之本，莫穷礼之旨。谓弓为弧⑥，则民不知矣；谓马为驷⑦，则民莫信矣。所以数乱于多，不乱于少；礼惑于大，不惑于小。能师于俭者，可以得其要。

·白话·

礼　要

　　礼仪，是由君王颁布的，但是君王并不清楚礼仪的原由；礼仪是由专门掌管礼仪的人负责的，但是这些人并不知道掌管的这些礼仪是什么。学问高深的儒士，居住在山林之中，尊敬老师和朋友，穷尽礼仪和舞乐，谈论"礼"的本旨与展开。一

①犹：通"由"
②棲山林：棲是指居住、停留。这里指栖居在山林之中，即隐居的意思。
③羽葆：仪仗名，以鸟羽为饰者。
④箫韶：相传舜的那个时代的乐器名。
⑤矍：老而勇健，形容人之精神很好。
⑥弧：木弓。
⑦驷：古代一车套四马，因以称四马之车或车之四马。

见到帝王的车马旌旗仪仗，就惊厥而起，像受到惊吓的鹿一样；一听见钟鼓琴箫的音乐声音，就怡然自得，像饱食终日无所事事的山猪一样。就像饮酒大醉，就像溺水那样手舞足蹈，也不清楚道的根本在哪里，也不去探求礼的要旨在哪里。把弓命名为弧，则众人都不知道弧是什么东西；把马命名为驷，则百姓都不知晓驷为何物。所以，礼数多了就会乱，礼数少了就不会乱；礼仪规模大了就会令人迷惑，小了就不会令人迷惑。能够以节俭为老师，就可以掌握礼仪的要旨。

Chapter 107

The Spirit of Rituals

The rituals are promulgated by emperors, but the emperors do not know the original reason for the rituals; the rituals are under the charge of designated people, but these officials do not know what these rituals are. The great scholars, who are highly learned, live in the mountains and forests, honor their teachers and friends, study rituals and music, and explore the nature and development of rituals. At the sight of the emperor's chariot, horses, flags etc, one rises up in fright, like a frightened deer; at the sound of the music of chims, drums harps and Xiao[1], one is happy, content and relaxed, like a mountain pig that has nothing to do on a full stomach. It is like drinking wine and getting drunk, like flailing when drowning in water. At this moment, people do not search for the root of the Tao, nor inquire the gist of the ritual. If you name a bow as an "Hu"[2], then none of the people know what a "Hu" is; if you name a horse as a "Si"[3], then none of the people know what a "Si" is. Therefore, if there are many rituals, it will be chaotic, but if there are few rituals, it will not be chaotic; if the ceremony is big, it will be confusing, but if it is simple, it will not be confusing. If you can take frugality as your teacher, you can grasp the essence of ritual.

---

①Xiao: A traditional Chinese musical instrument.

②Hu: It is another name for "bow".

③Si: It refers to a horse-drawn carriage.

· 原文 ·

清　静

奢者好动①，俭者好静；奢者好难，俭者好易；奢者好繁，俭者好简；奢者好逸乐，俭者好恬淡。有保一器毕生无璺②者，有挂一裘十年不毙者。斯人也可以亲百姓，可以司粟帛③，可以掌符玺④，可以即清静之道。

· 白话 ·

清　净

奢侈的人喜欢躁动交际，节俭的人喜欢清静；奢侈的人喜欢难得的东西，节俭的人喜欢容易得到的东西；奢侈的人喜欢繁复，节俭的人喜欢简单；奢侈的人喜欢安逸享乐，节俭的人喜欢恬淡闲适。有的人能一辈子使用陶瓷器物，却让陶瓷器物没有任何一点儿的裂纹，有的人能够让裘皮衣物挂上十年也毫不损坏。这样的人可以亲近百姓，可以掌管米粮布匹，可以掌握国家大权，可以跻身于清静大道。

---

① 动：躁动。

② 璺（wèn）：器皿的裂纹。

③ 粟帛：这里泛指粮食和布匹。

④ 符玺：兵符印玺。这里泛指国家政权。

Chapter 108

Peacefulness

Extravagant people like to be active and to socialize, while frugal people like to be quiet; extravagant people like rare things that are hard to get, while frugal people like things that are easy to get; extravagant people like complicated things, while frugal people like to have simple things; extravagant people like entertainment, while frugal people like to be quiet and peaceful. There are people who can use ceramic objects for a lifetime without making a single crack, and there are people who can have their fur clothes hung for ten years without causing any damage to these clothes. Such kinds of person can communicate with the common people and be close to them, take charge of a country's grain and cloth, hold the power of the state, and can be most close to peace and Taoism.

化书之 **109**

·原文·

损　益①

夫仁不俭，有不仁；义不俭，有不义；礼不俭，有非礼；智不俭，有无智；信不俭，有不信。所以知俭为五常之本，五常为俭之末。夫礼者，益之道也；俭者，损之道也。益者损之旨，损者益之理。礼过则淫，俭过则朴。自古及今，未有亡于俭者也。

·白话·

损　益

行仁爱之举的如果不节俭，就会产生不仁的事情；行义之举的如果不节俭，就会产生不义的事情；行礼仪之举的如果不节俭，就会产生违背礼仪的事情；行智谋之举的如果不节俭，就会出现愚蠢的事情；行诚信之举的如果不节俭，就会产生欺骗。所以，节俭为仁义礼智信这五常的根本所在，而五常则是节俭的末梢。礼仪，就是不断的增加，节俭，就是不停的减少。减损的要领目标在于增益，而指导增益的道理就是减损。礼多了就会过分，节俭多了则回归朴素。自古及今，还从来没有国家是由于节俭而亡国的。

---

① 损益：指减损或增加

Chapter 109

To Increase or Decrease

If those who perform acts of benevolence are not thrifty, they will certainly do things that are not benevolent; if those who perform acts of righteousness are not thrifty, they will certainly do things that are not righteous; if those who perform acts of ritual are not thrifty, they will certainly do things that violate ritual; if those who perform acts of wisdom are not thrifty, they will certainly do foolish things; if those who perform acts of integrity are not thrifty, they will certainly deceive. Therefore, thrift is the root of the Five Virtues of Benevolence, Righteousness, Ritual, Wisdom and Faithfulness, while the Five Virtues are the end branches of thrift. Ritual is to keep increasing, and frugality is to keep decreasing. The goal of reduction is to gain, and the way to gain is reduction. Excessive rituals lead to extravagance, and excessive frugality returns to simplicity. Since ancient times till today, no country has ever perished because of frugality.

化书之110

· 原文 ·

解　惑

谦者人所尊，俭者人所宝。使之谦必不谦，使之俭必不俭。我谦则民自谦，我俭则民自俭。机在此不在彼，柄在君不在人。恶行之者惑，是故为之文。

· 白话 ·

解　惑

谦虚的人被人尊重，节俭的人被人珍惜。强迫人们去谦虚的，人们肯定是不谦虚的；强迫人们去节俭的，人们肯定是不节俭的。君王谦虚了则百姓必然就谦虚，君王节俭了，百姓就必然会节俭。关键在于自己而不在于别人，根本在于君王而不在于百姓。恐怕想要践行这大道的人受惑，所以就写了这篇文章。

Chapter 110

Solutions to Confusing Behaviors

A humble person is respected, and a thrifty person is cherished. He who is forced to be modest is certainly not modest, and he who is forced to be frugal is certainly not frugal. If the emperor is modest, the people will be modest, and if the emperor is frugal, the people will be frugal. The key lies in oneself and not in others, and the root lies in the emperor and not in the people. I've written this because I worry that those who intend to practice this principal may be confused.